ROMANCING GOD

CHRISTIAN CLASSICS

ROMANCING GOD:

CONTEMPLATING THE BELOVED

RAMÓN LULL

Edited and Mildly Modernized by
HENRY L. CARRIGAN, JR.

PARACLETE PRESS
Brewster, Massachusetts

Library of Congress Cataloging-in-Publication Data

Llull, Ramon, 1232?-1316.
    Romancing God : contemplating the Beloved / Ramón Lull ; edited
and mildly modernized by Henry L. Carrigan, Jr.
        p.   cm.
    ISBN 1-55725-216-5 (pbk.)
    1. Mysticism—Spain—Early works to 1800. 2. Meditations.
I. Carrigan, Henry L., 1954-   . II. Llull, Ramon, 1232?-1316.
Llibre d'Amic e Amat. English. III. Llull, Ramon, 1232?-1316. Art
de contemplació. English. IV. Title.
BV5080.L566   1999
248.2'2—dc21   99-11223
                                                                        CIP

10 9 8 7 6 5 4 3 2 1

© *1999 by Paraclete Press*
ISBN 1-55725-216-5

Published by Paraclete Press
Brewster, Massachusetts
www.paraclete-press.com

Printed in the United States of America

Contents

Introduction

BIOGRAPHY

Although Ramon Lull (also Llull) was one of the greatest late medieval mystics, he was also an ardent missionary, fervently seeking the conversion of Muslims in a number of locales throughout Asia and Africa. In addition to his missionary activities, Lull was deeply devoted to philosophy, and all of his writings, including *The Book of the Lover and the Beloved* and *The Art of Contemplation,* reflect his attempt to combine deep spirituality with philosophical categories. According to one scholar, Lull sought to "relate all forms of knowledge . . . to the manifestations of the Divine Attributes in the universe." (This quotation is from *The Concise Oxford Dictionary of the Christian Church,* edited by E.A. Livingstone. Oxford, 1977, p. 311–12.) Though he had no formal degree or training in missiology or philosophy, he lectured widely in these subjects in Paris in 1287–1289, 1297–1299, and 1309–1311.

Lull was born to noble Catalan parents in Palma in Majorca, an island of the Balearic group and a possession of Spain, sometime between 1232 and 1235. When he was thirteen or fourteen, he became a knight in the court of King Don Jaime II. For the next eleven years or so, Lull lived the life of a courtier. Ruled by the chivalric code of honor, he protected his king and queen, but he also pursued a number of amorous relationships with the women of the court. During this period, he wrote numerous love poems in the tradition of courtly love poetry, anonymously praising and caressing his lovers in sexually charged language. His amorous pursuits led to his conversion at the age of thirty. As the story goes, Lull was so enamored of one of the court's women that he repeatedly asked her if he could lay his head on her bounteous breasts. She continued to refuse him, until one day she revealed to him her tumorous breast, black and eaten away with cancer. In that moment, so the story goes, Lull was converted to Christianity.

From his conversion till his death, Lull studied, wrote, and engaged in missionary activity. His missionary journeys took him to Asia (1276), Armenia (1302), and Africa (1280, 1292, 1306, 1314–1315). He promoted the study of languages as a preparation for effective missionary activity, and founded a language school at the Majorcan college of Miramar in 1276. Around 1275, he likely became involved in the religious life, studying with the Dominicans, and perhaps becoming a member of the Franciscan Third Order sometime between 1292 and 1295. Franciscan ideals of poverty and chastity certainly pervade his writings, including those contained in this volume. Lull produced well over three hundred works in both Catalan and Latin. In either 1282 or 1283, he began his *Blanquerna: A Thirteenth-Century Romance*, which contains *The Book of the Beloved* and *The Art of Contemplation*. On his final missionary journey to North Africa, Lull was stoned by a mob of Arabs, and according to many accounts, he died of his wounds in Tunis, in 1315.

Introduction

ROMANCING GOD

What appears in the present volume are two of Lull's most accessible mystical works, *The Book of the Lover and the Beloved* and *The Art of Contemplation*. The former is a grand, dazzling poem of love and adoration to God's almighty majesty. The latter is Lull's attempt to lay out as plainly as possible a method of contemplating God and His mercies and virtues.

The Book of the Lover and the Beloved is a collection of 365 short meditations that enable lovers of God to contemplate and adore their Beloved, God. In the prologue to the book, a Roman hermit discovers that many of his fellow hermits are not engaging properly in the contemplation and devotion of God. Thus, this hermit brings his concerns to the hermit Blanquerna, who has become famous for withdrawing from the world so that he may more ardently worship God. Blanquerna takes up the old hermit's request and produces *The Book of the Lover and the Beloved*.

"Far above lies the Beloved; far beneath it is the Lover; and love, which lies between these two, makes the Beloved descend to the Lover, and the Lover rise toward the Beloved." Thus Blanquerna describes the mystical journey. For Lull, the contemplative life has three stages. In the lowest stage, the intellect, or understanding, often acts as a hindrance to God's influence on the heart of the contemplative person. Here the will to love God is present, but the lover of God still has too much intellectual distraction to come completely into the ecstasy of God's embrace. In the penultimate stage, the contemplative has moved beyond the intellect to a state of semi-ecstasy. Although the senses often hinder the soul from union with God, this second stage is often described in sensual imagery. Finally, the soul experiences the ecstasy of union with God, its Beloved. This union, of course, is transient and ineffable, but it is toward this and that the Lover's will directs the soul's memory and understanding.

Lull's descriptions of the union of Lover and Beloved are drawn from the courtly love tradition of which he was so much a part as a young man. In this poetry, the lover is guided in all things by his lady's love. The beloved lady is often indifferent to the attentions of the lover, and the lover endures contempt and scorn, even as he remains devoted to his beloved. In *The Book of the Lover and the Beloved*, the soul takes the part of the adoring lover who seeks his beloved's attentions only to be tried by the torments of that love. Lull's sensual imagery captures this relationship: "The Lover and the Beloved met, and their caresses and embraces and kisses, their weeping and tears, bore witness to their meeting." The Lover also describes love as a "great affliction," yet concedes "what great happiness it is to love my Beloved." Lull uses the sensuous poetry of the court as a means of exalting the spiritual ecstasy of God's love.

In *The Art of Contemplation,* Lull seeks to provide the lover of God with a true method of contemplating God. As Blanquerna notes in the prologue to the book, "He started considering how he might make an art of contemplation that would lead him to have devotion in his heart, weeping and tears in his eyes, and help his will and understanding to rise higher to the contemplation of God's honors and wonders." Although this work is directed to contemplatives seeking an art whereby they can achieve union with God, Lull often waxes very philosophic in this writing. The book is divided into twelve parts, and several of the sections consider theological ideas using the philosophical language of substance, accidents, and essence so characteristic of medieval philosophy. The sections on "Essence," "Unity," "Trinity," and "Incarnation" evoke imagery of the contemplation of God even as they delve into the mystery of the transubstantiation of Christ's divine and human natures. Lull also uses the *Pater Noster* and the *Ave Maria* as paths down which contemplatives might journey toward God. Finally, Lull explores the Divine Virtues of Goodness, Greatness, Eternity, Power, Wisdom, Love, Virtue, Truth, Glory, Perfection, Justice, Liberality, Mercy, Humility, Dominion, and Patience. He closes his book on the art of contemplation by considering the seven deadly sins and the ways that the Divine Virtues, truly contemplated, enable souls to overcome these sins.

Lull combines the theological sophistication of Bonaventure and the passion and devotion of Francis of Assisi in his writing. As in Bonaventure, the contemplative mind undertakes a journey toward the ecstatic union of heart and mind with the God who is omnipotent and almighty. As in Francis, the fool of love, the poor man of Christ, renounces all worldly passions and desires as he seeks ecstatic union with the Beloved Divine object. As one scholar has so aptly put it: "Lull is the follower of the poor Christ; the court fool for human kings; the court troubadour and sweet singer of God's praises in the heavenly mansion; the knight of the poor Lord and the gracious Lady." [This quotation comes from *Late Medieval Mysticism*, edited by Ray Petry. Philadelphia: Westminster, 1957. p. 147.]

A WORD ABOUT THE TEXT

The text of *The Book of the Lover and the Beloved* and *The Art of Contemplation* are taken from *Blanquerna: A Thirteenth Century Romance*, translated by E. Allison Peers, London: Jarrolds, 1925.

I have remained true to the spirit of the text, even where I have mildly modernized it. Mostly, my modernizations have come in three areas. First, I have replaced archaic words and forms of address with more modern ones. Thus "Thou" becomes "You" throughout. Second, I have attempted to use inclusive language in this edition. I have retained the masculine pronouns for God, so as not to be anachronistic. But, wherever Lull speaks of individuals in a generic fashion, I have replaced "man" with "humanity" or "humankind." Finally, I have altered the syntax and the sentence structure of the writing to make it livelier and more appealing to a contemporary audience. Most often this simply means casting sentences in the active rather than the passive voice.

I hope this edition of Lull's writing will introduce his lyrical spirituality to a whole new group of lovers of God.

THE BOOK
OF THE LOVER AND
THE BELOVED

CHAPTER ONE
Prologue

One day a Roman hermit visited the other hermits in Rome, and he discovered that they had many temptations, mainly because they did not know how to live in a manner devoted to God. So the hermit went to the famous contemplative hermit Blanquerna, and asked him to write a book that would teach the hermits the arts of contemplation and devotion.

Blanquerna thought a long time about how he would write the book and what kinds of subjects it should contain. After a time of thinking, he gave himself fervently to the adoration and contemplation of God, so that in prayer God would show him how he should write this book. While Blanquerna wept and adored, God caused his soul to rise to its supreme heights in contemplation of Him. Carried away by the fervor of his devotion, Blanquerna realized that love is strong and boundless when the Lover passionately loves his Beloved. Thus, it occurred to Blanquerna to write a book of the Lover and the Beloved, in which the Lover should be the faithful and devout Christian, and the Beloved should be God.

While Blanquerna was praying, he thought about ways of contemplating God and His virtues. When he finished praying, he wrote down the manner in which he had contemplated God. He did this daily, so that many diverse ways of contemplating God would be included in *The Book of the Lover and the Beloved.* Blanquerna wished to keep these instructions brief so that in a short time the soul could learn to reflect many ways of contemplating God. With God's blessing, Blanquerna began to write his book, dividing it into as many verses as there are days in the year, each verse sufficient for the contemplation of God in one day.

CHAPTER TWO
The Contemplative Verses

1. So great was his love for the Beloved, the Lover wondered whether or not there remained anything in the Beloved still to love. When he asked the Beloved this question, the Beloved told the Lover that he still had to love those things that could increase his own love.

2. The paths the Lover travels as he seeks the Beloved are long and perilous, marked by sighs and tears, but they are lighted by love.

3. Many lovers came to love their Beloved, the One who blessed them with overflowing love. Each one had the Beloved for his possession, and his thoughts of Him were very pleasant.

4. The Lover wept and said: "How long will it be until the darkness of the world is past, and the paths to hell are gone? When will there be more innocent people than guilty people in the world?"

5. "When will the Lover lay down his life for the Beloved? And when will the Beloved see the Lover grow faint out of love of Him?"

6. The Lover said to the Beloved: "You who fill the sun with its splendor, fill my heart with love." The Beloved answered: "If you weren't already filled with love, you would not be weeping, and you would not have come to this place to see the One who loves you."

7. To see if the Lover's love for Him was perfect, the Beloved asked the Lover how the Beloved's presence differed from His absence. The Lover replied: "As

knowledge and remembrance differ from ignorance and oblivion."

8.   The Beloved asked the Lover: "Do you remember any rewards I have given you that would cause you to love Me so fervently?" "Yes," said the Lover, "because I do not distinguish between the trials and the joys that You give me."

9.   So the Beloved asked: "If I double your trials, will you still be patient?" The Lover answered: "Yes, so You may double also my love."

10. The Beloved said to the Lover: "Do you know yet know what love means?" The Lover replied: "If I didn't know the meaning of love, I would certainly know the meaning of trial, grief, and sorrow."

11. His enemies asked the Lover: "Why don't you answer your Beloved when He calls you?" The Lover said: "To come to Him, I endure great perils and I ask for His grace when I speak to Him."

12. "Foolish Lover!" they said, "why do you give up all your wealth and the joys of this world to be an outcast among people?" The Lover replied: "I do this to honor my Beloved, who is unloved and dishonored by more people than honor and love Him."

13. "Say, Fool of Love! Is it easier to see the Beloved in the Lover or to see the Lover in the Beloved?" The Lover answered: "You can know the Beloved by love and the Lover by sighs and tears and trials and grief."

14. The Lover tried to find someone who would tell the Beloved all the great trials he was enduring for the sake of His love. The Lover found his Beloved reading a book in which He had written all the griefs and

trials the Lover's love made him suffer for his Beloved as well as the joy that this love brought him.

15. Our Lady presented her Son to the Lover, so he might kiss His feet, and write about Our Lady's virtues in his book.

16. The Lover said to the singing bird: "Have you placed yourself in my Beloved's care so He will protect you from indifference and make your love for Him greater?" The bird replied: "Who makes me sing but the Lord of love, Who calls indifference a sin?"

17. Love makes her home between fear and hope. Love lives on thought and dies of forgetfulness, which marks the delight of this world.

18. The eyes and the memory of the Lover argued about whether or not it was better to see the Beloved than to remember Him. Memory said that remembrance brings tears to the eyes, making the heart burn with love.

19. The Lover asked Understanding and Will which was closer to his Beloved. The two had a race, and Understanding came closer to the Beloved than Will.

20. Once there was strife between the Lover and the Beloved. Seeing the strife, another lover wept until the Beloved and Lover made peace.

21. Sighs and Tears came to the Beloved and asked Him which of them loved Him more deeply. The Beloved told them that sighs were closer to love and tears closer to the eyes.

22. The Lover came and drank of the fountain that gives love to those who have no love, and the Lover's griefs were redoubled. The Beloved came to drink from the

same fountain so His love for the Lover might be doubled.

23. The Lover was sick, so he contemplated the Beloved. The Beloved fed him on His merits, quenched his thirst with love, made him rest in patience, clothed him with humility, and gave him truth as medicine.

24. They asked the Lover where his Beloved could be found. The Lover answered: "Look for yourselves and see Him in a house nobler than the nobility of all creation; you can see Him, too, in my love, my griefs, and my tears."

25. They asked the Lover: "Where are you going?" He answered: "I am coming from my Beloved." They asked: "When are you coming?" "I go to my Beloved," he said. "When will you return?" "I shall be with my Beloved," he said. "How long will you be with your Beloved?" "I will be with Him for as long as my thoughts remain on Him," said the Lover.

26. The birds welcomed the dawn with their songs, and the Lover, who is the dawn, awakened. When the birds ended their songs, the Lover died in the dawn for his Beloved.

27. In the orchard, the bird sang of the Beloved. The Lover came and said to the bird: "Even though we don't understand one another's speech, love helps us to understand one another. In your song I see my Beloved."

28. Although he was weary from his labors in seeking his Beloved, the Lover was afraid to fall asleep and forget Him. So the Lover wept so that he could stay awake and remember his Beloved.

29. The Lover and the Beloved met, and the Beloved said: "You don't need to speak to Me. Signal Me with your eyes, for they are words to My heart, and I will give you what you ask."

30. The Lover wept because he was disobedient to his Beloved. So the Beloved appeared in the form of His Lover, and died, so the Lover could regain what he had lost. So He gave him a greater gift than the one he had lost.

31. The Beloved filled His Lover with love, and didn't grieve over the Lover's trials, since they made the Lover love the Beloved more deeply. The greater the Lover's trials, the greater was his joy.

32. The Lover said: "The secrets of my Beloved torture me, for my deeds reveal them, and my mouth keeps silence and reveals them to none."

33. This is Love's contract: Love must be patient, humble, fearful, diligent, and trustful; he must be ready to face great dangers for the honor of his Beloved. The Beloved, in turn, must be true and free, merciful and just, with His Lover.

34. The Lover looked all over the earth for true devotion, to see if his Beloved were well served. So he went below ground to see if he could find more perfect devotion, which was lacking above ground.

35. The Lover asked the bird: "Please ask my Beloved, Whose servant I am, why He tortures me with love." The bird replied: "If you did not suffer trials for Love, how could you show your Love for Him?"

36. In deep thought, the Lover walked the paths of his Beloved. He stumbled and fell among thorns, but they felt to him like flowers and a bed of love.

37. They asked the Lover: "Would you trade your Beloved for another?" The Lover answered: "Why? There is no other who is better or nobler than the sovereign and eternal Good. He is infinite in greatness and power and wisdom and love and perfection."

38. The Lover wept and sang of his Beloved: "Love in the heart of the lover is swifter than the splendor of lightning to the eye. Love's tears gather more swiftly than the waves of the sea, and sighing is more proper to love than whiteness is to snow."

39. They asked the Lover: "In what lies the glory of your Beloved?" He answered: "He is Power itself." They asked: "In what lies His wisdom?" He replied: "He is Wisdom itself." They asked: "And why is He to be loved?" The Lover said: "Because He is Love itself."

40. The Lover rose early and went in search of his Beloved. As he met other travelers, he asked them if they had seen his Beloved. They asked: "When did you lose sight of your Beloved?" The Lover answered: "Even when my Beloved is not in my thoughts, He is never absent from my sight, because everything I see is a picture of my Beloved."

41. The Lover gazed upon the Beloved with eyes of thought and grief, sighs and tears, and the Beloved gazed upon the Lover with eyes of grace, justice and pity, mercy and bounty.

42. The keys of the doors of love are decorated with meditations, sighs, and tears. The cord that binds them is woven of conscience, contrition, devotion, and satisfaction. The door is kept by justice and mercy.

43. The Lover knocked with love and hope on the

Beloved's door. With humility, pity, charity, and patience, the Beloved heard the knocking of His Lover. Deity and Humanity opened the doors, and the Lover went in to his Beloved.

44. Propriety and Community met and joined together so that there could be love and benevolence between Lover and Beloved.

45. Two fires nurture the love of the Lover. One is made of pleasures, desires, and thoughts. The other is made of fear and grief, weeping and tears.

46. The Lover longed for solitude, and went away to live alone so he could have the companionship of his Beloved.

47. The Lover sat alone in the shade of a tree. When people passed him, they asked why he was alone. The Lover answered: "I am alone, not that I have seen and heard you; until now, I was in the company of my Beloved."

48. By signs of love, the Lover talked with the Beloved. By means of fear, of weeping and tears, and of thoughts, the Lover told the Beloved of his griefs.

49. The Lover was afraid that his Beloved might take His love from His Lover. But with a contrite heart the Lover repented of his fear, and the Beloved restored hope and compassion to the Lover's heart, and weeping and tears to his eyes, so love would return to the Lover.

50. Distance does not matter to the Lover and the Beloved, for their love mingles as water mingles with wine. They are linked like heat and light, and they are united as Essence and Being.

51. The Lover said to the Beloved: "I find my healing and my grief in You. The more You heal me, the greater grows my grief, and the more I languish, the more health You give me." The Beloved answered: "Your love is a kind of badge with which you show My honor before men."

52. The Lover imagined himself bound, wounded, and killed for the sake of his Beloved. Those who tortured him asked: "Where is your Beloved?" He replied: "You can see Him in the increase of my love and the strength it gives me to bear these tortures."

53. The Lover said to the Beloved: "I have never left You or ceased to love You since I knew You. I have always been by You wherever I went." The Beloved answered: "And I have never failed you or forgotten you or deceived you since you have known and loved Me."

54. Like one who had lost his wits, the Lover walked through a city, singing of his Beloved. When people asked him if he had lost his wits, he replied: "My Beloved has taken my will, and I have yielded to Him my understanding. I have nothing left but my memory, which I use to remember my Beloved."

55. The Beloved said: "It would be a miracle if the Lover fell asleep and forgot his Beloved." The Lover replied: "It would also be a miracle if the Beloved did not wake up the sleeping Lover, since He has desired him."

56. The Lover's heart soared to the height of the Beloved, so that he would not be hindered from loving Him in this world. When he reached the Beloved, the Lover

contemplated Him with delight and sweetness. But the Beloved led the Lover down to this world so that he might contemplate Him in griefs and trials.

57. They asked the Lover: "In what lies your wealth?" He answered: "In the poverty that I bear for my Beloved." They asked: "Where is your repose?" He answered: "In the afflictions of love." They asked: "Who is your physician?" He replied: "The trust I have in my Beloved." They asked : "Who is your master?" He said: "The signs of the Beloved I see in all creatures."

58. As the bird sang upon a flowering tree, the Lover asked the bird: "What do the trembling of the leaves and the scent of flowers mean?" The bird answered: "The trembling of the leaves signifies obedience, and the scent of the flowers signifies suffering and adversity."

59. The Lover met two friends who greeted, embraced, and kissed each other, with love and tears. So strongly did this scene recall the Beloved to his memory that the Lover almost fainted.

60. Contemplating dying and death, the Lover was filled with fear until he remembered his Beloved. He cried in a loud voice to everyone near him: "Have love so you may fear neither death nor danger as you do honor my Beloved."

61. They asked the Lover where his love first began. He replied: "It began in the glories of my Beloved. From such a beginning I began to love my neighbor as myself and to hate deception and falsehood."

62. They said: "Fool of love! What would you do if your Beloved no longer loved you?" "I would still love him,"

he replied, "for not to love is death, and love is life."

63. They asked the Lover what he meant by perseverance. He answered: "It is both happiness and sorrow in the Lover who loves, honors, and serves his Beloved with fortitude, patience, and hope."

64. The Lover asked his Beloved to repay him for the time he had served the Beloved. So the Beloved added up the thoughts, tears, longings, perils, and trials the Lover had endured for His love, and the Beloved added eternal bliss to the account and gave Himself as a repayment to His Lover.

65. They asked the Lover what he meant by happiness. He answered: "It is sorrow endured for the sake of Love."

66. They said: "Fool of love! What do you think sorrow means?" He replied: "Sorrow is the memory of the dishonor done to my Beloved, who is worthy of all honor."

67. The Lover gazed on a Place where he had seen his Beloved and said: "Will you tell my Beloved that I suffer trials and sorrows for His sake?" Place replied: "When your Beloved hung upon me, He endured for your love greater trials and sorrows than all other trials and sorrows Love could give its servants."

68. The Lover said to his Beloved: "You are all, and through all, and in all, and with all. I would give You all of myself so I could have all of You, and You all of me." The Beloved answered: "You cannot have Me wholly unless you belong entirely to Me." So the Lover said: "Let me be wholly Yours and You be wholly mine." The Beloved said: "What then will your son, your brother, and your father have?" The Lover

replied: "You, my Beloved, are so great a Whole that You can be wholly of each one who gives himself wholly to You."

69. The Lover contemplated the greatness of his Beloved and found in Him neither beginning nor end. The Beloved asked: "What are you measuring?" The Lover answered: "I measure the lesser with the greater, defect with fullness, and beginning with infinity and eternity, so humility, patience, love, and hope may be planted more firmly in my remembrance."

70. Love's paths are long and short. Love is clear, bright and pure, subtle yet simple, strong, diligent, brilliant, and abounding in fresh thought and old memories.

71. They asked the Lover; "What are the fruits of love?" He answered: "Love's fruits are pleasures, thoughts, desires, longings, sighs, trials, perils, torments, and griefs. Without these fruits Love's servants have no part in her."

72. The Lover complained that the Beloved did not increase his love and that Love gave him trials and sorrows. The Beloved told him that the trials and sorrows were the increase of love itself.

73. They asked: "Why don't you speak, and why are you thoughtful and perplexed?" The Lover answered: "I am contemplating the beauties of my Beloved as well as the likeness between the joys and sorrows given to me by Love."

74. They asked: "Was your heart or your love created first?" The Lover replied: "My heart and my love were created together, for the heart was made for love and love for reflection."

75. They asked: "Was your love born in the secrets of the Beloved or in the revelation of those secrets to men?" The Lover answered: "Love makes no such distinction. Secretly, the Lover keeps hidden the Beloved's secrets, and secretly, he also reveals them. Yet, when they are revealed he keeps them secret still."

76. Unrevealed, love's secrets bring anguish and grief; revealed, love brings fervor and fear. Because of this, the Lover is always sorrowful.

77. Love called his lovers and told them to ask from him the most desirable and pleasing gifts. They asked Love to dress them in his own clothes, so they might be more acceptable in the Beloved's eyes.

78. The Lover called out to everyone: "Love commands you always to love: in waking and sleeping, in joy and sorrow, in gain and in loss. In whatever you do, you must love; for this is Love's first commandment."

79. They asked, "Fool of Love! When did you first meet Love?" The Lover replied: "I first met Love when my heart was filled with thoughts and desires, sighs and griefs, and my eyes were filled with tears. Through my memory and understanding, Love taught me the wonderful ways of my Beloved. I received Love's teachings with love and hope, and I harbor Love's teachings in my heart with strength and wisdom."

80. The Beloved sang: "The Lover does not know love very well if he is ashamed to praise his Beloved or is afraid to honor Him in places where He is dishonored. If the Lover is impatient in his trials, he knows little of love."

81. The Lover sent letters to his Beloved, asking Him if

there was anyone who would help him suffer and bear the trials that he endured for Him. The Beloved replied: "I will not fail or deceive you."

82. They asked the Beloved about His love of the Lover, and He replied: "My love is a mingling of joy and sorrow, fervor and fear."

83. They asked the Lover about the love of his Beloved, and he answered: "The love that flows from the Beloved to the Lover is eternal and perfect, and full of infinite goodness and wisdom."

84. They asked the Fool of Love: "What would you say is marvelous about love?" He said: "It is a marvel to me that people love absent things more than present things, and they love visible and corruptible things more than invisible and incorruptible things."

85. As the Lover was seeking his Beloved, he found a man who was dying without love, and he said: "It is profoundly sad that any person should die without love. Why are you dying without love?" The man answered: "Because I have lived without love."

86. The Lover asked his Beloved: "What is greater—loving, or love itself?" The Beloved said: "In creatures, love is the tree, the tree's fruit is loving, and the tree's flowers and leaves are trials and griefs. In God, love and loving are one and the same thing, without either trials or griefs."

87. As the result of too much thinking, the Lover was grieving and sorrowful. He begged his Beloved to send him a book that might reveal the Beloved's virtues and relieve the Lover's sorrow. So the Beloved sent that book to His Lover, and his trials and griefs were doubled.

88. The Lover was sick with love. The physician who came to see him multiplied his sorrows and thoughts, and in that same hour the Lover was healed.

89. Love and the Lover celebrated the joy of the Beloved, and the Beloved revealed himself to them. The Lover cried and went into an ecstatic trance, and Love fainted. The Beloved brought His Lover to life by reminding him of His virtues.

90. The Lover said to the Beloved: "There are many ways You reveal yourself to my heart and my sight. I call You by many names, but the love by which You refresh and humiliate me is one, and one alone."

91. The Beloved revealed Himself to His Lover. He stretched out His Arms to embrace him and bent His Head to kiss him. The Beloved remained on high so that the Lover would always seek Him.

92. The Beloved was absent from His Lover, and the Lover sought the Beloved with his memory and understanding, so he could love Him. When the Lover found the Beloved, he asked Him where He had been. The Beloved answered: "In the absence of your memory and in the ignorance of your understanding."

93. They asked the Fool of Love: "Aren't you ashamed when people see you cry for your Beloved?" "Sin without shame," said the Lover, "indicates a defect of love in those who do not know how to love."

94. The Beloved planted sighs and longings, virtues and love in the heart of the Lover. The Lover watered the seeds with his tears.

95. The Beloved planted trials and griefs in the body of

the Lover. The Lover cultivated his body with hope, devotion, and patience.

96. The Beloved held a great feast, inviting many rich men and giving great gifts. When the Lover came to this feast, the Beloved asked: "Who invited you to this feast?" The Lover replied: "Need and love compelled me to attend, so I might see Your splendid glory and Your wonder."

97. They asked the Lover: "From where did you come?" He answered: "From love." "To whom do you belong?" "I belong to love." "Who gave you birth?" "Love." "Where were you born?" "In love." "Who raised you?" "Love." "How do you live?" "By love." "What is your name?" "Love." "Where do you go?" "To love." "Where do you dwell?" "In love." "Do you have anything but love?" they asked. "Yes," he answered, "I have faults, and I have sins against my Beloved." "Will your Beloved forgive you?" they asked. "Yes," said the Lover, "my Beloved is full of mercy and justice."

98. The Beloved left the Lover. The Lover looked for Him in his thoughts and used the language of love to ask others if they had seen the Beloved.

99. The Lover found his Beloved, Who was despised among the people. When the Lover told the Beloved how people dishonored Him, the Beloved said: "I suffer such dishonor because I lack devoted and fervent lovers." The Lover cried, and his sorrows were increased. But, the Beloved comforted him, revealing His wonders to him.

100. The light of the Beloved's abode illumined the Lover's

dwelling and filled it with joys and griefs and thoughts. So that the Beloved could reside there, the Lover threw out all things from his dwelling.

101. They asked the Lover what sign his Beloved bore upon His banner. He answered: "The sign of One dead." They asked him why He bore such a sign. The Lover said: "Because He once died, and because those who glory in being His lovers must follow in His steps."

102. When the Beloved came to visit His Lover's dwelling, the Lover's steward demanded payment. But the Lover said: "My Beloved is to stay here without payment."

103. Memory and Will climbed into the mountain of the Beloved, so understanding could be exalted and love for the Beloved increased.

104. Every day sighs and tears are messengers between the Lover and the Beloved, so between them there will be solace, companionship, friendship, and goodwill.

105. The Lover yearned for his Beloved, and he sent Him his thoughts so they could bring bliss from his Beloved.

106. The Beloved gave His Lover the gift of tears, sighs, griefs, thoughts, and sorrows. With these gifts the Lover served the Beloved.

107. The Lover begged his Beloved to give him riches, peace, and honor in this world. The Beloved revealed His Face to the memory and understanding of the Lover, and made Himself the Goal of the Lover's will.

108. They asked the Lover: "In what does honor consist?" He replied: "In comprehending and loving my Beloved." They also asked him: "In what lies dishon-

or?" He answered: "In forgetting and ceasing to love Him."

109. "I was tormented by love, O Beloved, until I exclaimed that You were present in my torments. Love then eased my griefs, and as a reward You increased my love and love doubled my torments.

110. The Lover met another on the path of love who reproached Love with tears and grief. Love defended Himself with loyalty, hope, devotion, and happiness. Love decried the Lover for his reproaches, since He had given the Lover such noble gifts.

111. The Lover sang: "Ah, what great affliction love is! Ah, what great happiness it is to love my Beloved, Who loves His lovers with infinite and eternal love, perfect and complete."

112. On his way into a far country to find his Beloved, the Lover met two lions. The Lover was afraid of death, because he wanted to live and serve his Beloved. He sent Memory to his Beloved, so Love could be with him at death and help him endure death. While the Lover remembered his Beloved, the two lions came humbly to him, licked his tears, and caressed his hands and feet. So the Lover continued searching for his Beloved.

113. The Lover journeyed far and wide, but he could not escape the prison of Love in which his body and thoughts, desires, and joys had been captive.

114. While the Lover was working in this way, he came across a hermit sleeping near a spring. Waking the hermit, the Lover asked him if he had seen the Beloved in his dreams. The hermit answered that,

sleeping or waking, he was held captive in a prison of love. The lover rejoiced that he had found a fellow-prisoner. They both cried, because the Beloved has few lovers like these.

115. There is nothing in the Beloved that does not give the Lover care and sorrow. And the Lover experiences no pain that does not come from the Beloved and give Him joy. Therefore the Beloved's love is always in action, while the Lover's love ever brings him grief and suffering.

116. A bird singing on a branch said: "I will give the Lover a fresh thought, and he will give me two." The bird gave the thought to the Lover, and the Lover gave two to the bird, so it would be comforted, and the Lover felt his griefs increased.

117. The Lover and the Beloved met, and their caresses, kisses, and tears testified to their love for one another. When the Beloved asked the Lover about his state, the Lover was speechless.

118. The Lover and the Beloved struggled together, and their love made peace between them. Which of the two, do you think, possessed the stronger love toward the other?

119. The Lover loved all those who feared his Beloved, and he feared all those who did not fear Him. Was love or fear greater in the Lover?

120. The Lover followed his Beloved, and he passed along a road where there was a fierce lion that killed everyone who passed by it carelessly and without devotion.

121. The Lover said: "The people who do not fear my Beloved must fear all things, and those who do fear

Him may be bold and fervent in all things."

122. The Lover said: "One's motives must be to have pleasure in penance, understanding in knowledge, hope in patience, health in abstinence, consolation in remembrance, love in diligence, loyalty in shame, riches in poverty, peace in obedience, and strife in malevolence."

123. Love shone through the cloud that had come between the Lover and the Beloved, and it made the cloud as bright as the moon is at night and as brilliant as the midday sun. Through the bright cloud the Lover and the Beloved talked together.

124. They asked the Lover: "What is the greatest darkness?" He answered: "My Beloved's absence." "And what is the greatest light?" they asked. He replied: "My Beloved's presence."

125. The Beloved's sign can be seen in the Lover, who experiences trials, sighs, and tears, and people's contempt for the sake of love.

126. The Lover wrote: "My Beloved is happy because I raise my thoughts to Him, and my eyes cry for Him; without grief I have neither life nor feeling."

127. "O Understanding and Will, wake up the watchdogs that are asleep and have forgotten my Beloved. Memory, do not forget the dishonor done to my Beloved by those whom He has honored."

128. The enmity between people and my Beloved increases. My Beloved promises gifts and rewards, and threatens with justice and wisdom. Memory and Will despise His threats and His promises.

129. As the Beloved came to comfort the Lover for his

griefs, the Lover grieved more, exclaiming that many people dishonored the Beloved.

130. With the pen of love, with the water of his tears, and on the paper of suffering, the Lover wrote letters to his Beloved. In the letters, he told how love was dying and how sin and error were increasing the number of His enemies.

131. Memory, understanding, and will bound the Lover and the Beloved, and the cord binding these two loves was woven of thoughts and griefs, sighs and tears.

132. The Lover lay in the bed of love: His sheets were made from joys, his quilt made from griefs, and his pillow made from tears. No one could tell if the fabric of the pillow was the fabric from the sheet or the quilt.

133. The Beloved clothed his Lover's body with thoughts, his feet with trials, and his head with a garland of tears.

134. The Beloved entreated His Lover not to forget Him. The Lover replied that he could not forget Him because he could not do otherwise than to know Him.

135. The Beloved said to the Lover: "You shall praise and defend Me where people fail to praise Me." The Lover answered: "Provide me with love." The Beloved replied: "Because I love you so much, I became incarnate and endured pains of death."

136. The Lover said to the Beloved: "Show me how I can make You known, loved, and praised among all people." The Beloved filled His Lover with devotion,

patience, compassion, trials, and tears. The Lover's heart was filled with boldness to praise his Beloved, and his mouth was full of praises of the Beloved. The Lover was contemptuous of the reproaches of those who judge falsely.

137. The Lover spoke to the people: "The one who truly remembers my Beloved forgets all earthly things; the one who forgets all things in remembering my Beloved is defended from all things by Him and receives a part in all things."

138. They asked the Lover: "How is Love born, how does it live, and how does it die?" The Lover answered: "Love is born of remembrance, lives on understanding, and dies through forgetfulness."

139. The Lover forgot all earthly things so his understanding could soar toward a knowledge of the Beloved, Whom he wanted to contemplate and preach.

140. The Lover went to fight for the honor of his Beloved and armed himself with faith, hope, love, justice, and courage so he could defeat the Beloved's enemies. The Lover would have been defeated, though, if the Beloved had not helped declare His greatness.

141. The Lover wanted to reach the farthest goal of love for his Beloved, but other objects blocked his path. Because of this, the Lover's longings and desires gave him sorrow and grief.

142. The Lover rejoiced in the greatness of his Beloved, but he was sad because of too much reflection. He didn't know whether he felt joy or sorrow more deeply.

143. The Beloved sent His Lover to Christian princes and

unbelievers to teach them an art of contemplation so they could know and love the Beloved.

144. If you see a lover clothed in fine clothes, honored through vanity, gorged with food and sleep, in that person you see damnation and torment. If you see a lover poorly clothed, pale from fasting, in that person you see salvation and everlasting joy.

145. The Lover cried out for the heat of love that he had within him. The Lover died, and the Beloved wept, and comforted him with patience, hope, and reward.

146. The Lover wept for what he had lost; no one could comfort him, for he could not regain his losses.

147. God created the night, so the Lover could keep vigil and contemplate the glories of his Beloved. The Lover thought God created the night for the rest of those wearied with loving.

148. People mocked the Lover, because he acted as a fool for love's sake. The Lover despised and admonished them because they did not love his Beloved.

149. The Lover said: "Though I am dressed in vile clothing, love clothes my heart with thoughts of delight and my body with tears and sufferings."

150. The Beloved sang: "Those that praise Me devote themselves to praising My worth, and My enemies torment them and hold them in contempt. Thus, I have sent My Lover to lament My dishonor, and his laments and tears are born of My love."

151. The Lover told the Beloved that for His sake he endured and loved trials and sufferings, and he begged the Beloved to love him and have compassion on his trials and sufferings. The Beloved replied that

it was His nature to love all those who loved Him and to have pity on those who endured trials for His sake. The Lover rejoiced in the nature of his Beloved.

152. The Beloved silenced His Lover, and the Lover took comfort in gazing upon his Beloved.

153. The Lover cried and called for his Beloved, until the Beloved descended from the supreme heights of Heaven. He came to earth to weep and grieve and die for the sake of love, and to teach people to know and love and praise His honors.

154. The Lover reproached Christians, because in their letters they do not put first the name of his Beloved, Jesus Christ.

155. The Lover met a squire who was pale, thin, pensive, and poorly clothed. The squire greeted the Lover and said: "May God guide you so you may find your Beloved." When the Lover asked how the squire had recognized him, he said: "Some of Love's secrets reveal others, so lovers recognize one another."

156. The Beloved's good works and glories are the Lover's riches. The Beloved's treasures are the thoughts, desires, torments, tears, and griefs with which the Lover honors and loves his Beloved.

157. Great numbers of lovers have gathered together, and they bear the banner of love that displays the sign of their Beloved. All of them will possess love, so their Beloved will not be dishonored.

158. People who show their foolishness by gathering riches move the Lover to be a fool for love, and the shame the Lover feels at being a fool brings him esteem and

love. Which of these two emotions is the greater occasion of love?

159. The Lover became sad through an excess of thought. The Beloved sang, and the Lover rejoiced to hear Him. Which of these two occasions gave the Lover a greater increase of love?

160. The Beloved's secrets are revealed in the Lover's secrets, and the Lover's secrets are revealed in the Beloved's secrets. Which of these two secrets is the greater occasion of revelation?

161. They asked the Fool of Love by what signs they might know his Beloved. He answered: "By mercy and pity, which are in His Will."

162. So great was the Lover's love for the Beloved that he wished for the good of all people above the good of the individual, and for his Beloved to be known, praised, and desired everywhere.

163. Love and Indifference met in a garden where the Lover and the Beloved were talking in secret. Love asked Indifference why he had come to the garden. "So the Lover may cease loving and the Beloved may cease to be honored," he replied. Indifference's words displeased the Beloved and the Lover, and their love increased, so it could defeat Indifference.

164. "Say, Fool of Love. Do you take greater pleasure in loving or hating?" "In loving," he replied, "for I have hated only so that I may love more."

165. "Say, Fool of Love. Do you try to understand truth or falsehood better?" He answered: "Truth." They asked: "Why?" He replied: "I understand falsehood so I may better understand truth."

166. The Lover realized how greatly the Beloved loved him, and he asked Him if His love and His mercy were one and the same. The Beloved replied that in His Essence there was no distinction between love and mercy. So the Lover said: Why does Your love torment me, and why doesn't Your mercy heal my griefs?" The Beloved answered: "My mercy gives you these griefs so you may more perfectly honor My love."

167. When the Lover wanted to go into a strange country to do honor to his Beloved, he tried to disguise himself so he wouldn't be taken captive. But he could not hide his tears, sighs, sorrows, and griefs. So he was captured and tormented by his Beloved's enemies.

168. The Lover was imprisoned in the prison of Love. He was chained in thoughts, desires, and memories so he would not flee to his Beloved. Griefs tormented him; patience and hope consoled him. The Lover would have died, but the Beloved revealed His Presence, and the Lover revived.

169. When the Lover met his Beloved, he recognized Him and wept. The Beloved reproved him, because the Lover did not cry until he recognized Him. The Beloved asked: "When did you first recognize Me, since you were not already weeping?" The Lover replied: "I knew You in my memory, understanding, and will, but as soon as I saw You with my eyes, my love increased."

170. "What do you mean by love?" said the Beloved. The Lover answered: "It is to carry in my heart the Beloved's features and words. It is the yearning in my heart, with desire and tears."

171. "Love is the mingling of boldness and fear that comes through great fervor. It is the desire of the Beloved as the goal of the will. It makes the Lover die when he hears one sing of the beauties of the Beloved. In love I die daily, and love is forever my will."

172. Devotion and Yearning sent thoughts as messengers to the Lover's heart, to bring tears to his eyes, which had wept for a long time but which would now weep no more.

173. The Lover said to all who love: "If you want fire, come light your lanterns at my heart; if you want water, come to my eyes, for the tears flow in streams; if you want thoughts of love, come gather them from my meditations."

174. One day the Lover was meditating on his great love for the Beloved and the great trials into which this love had led him. As he was considering how great his rewards would be, he remembered that his Beloved had already rewarded him by kindling within him a love for His Presence.

175. The Lover was wiping away the tears he had shed for Love's sake, since he was afraid to reveal the sufferings his Beloved had sent him. The Beloved said: "Why would you hide these marks of My love from others? I gave them to you so others may also love Me."

176. They asked: "How long will you, who appear as a fool for the sake of love, be a slave, forced to weep and suffer trials and griefs?" He answered: "Until my Beloved separates my body from my soul."

177. They exclaimed: "Fool of Love, do you have riches?"

He replied: "I have my Beloved." "Do you have towns, cities, castles, or provinces?" The Lover answered: "I have love, thoughts, tears, desires, trials, and griefs, which are better than empires or kingdoms."

178. They asked the Lover how he recognized his Beloved's decrees. He answered: "Because in them He gives equality of joys and griefs to His lovers."

179. They asked: "Fool of Love, who knows more of love—the one who has joys because of love or the one who has trials and griefs because of love?" He answered: "There can be no knowledge of love without both one and the other."

180. They asked the Lover: "Why won't you defend yourself from sins and false crimes of which people accuse you?" He replied: "I have to defend my Beloved, whom people falsely accuse; people may indeed be full of deceit and error, and are not worthy of being defended."

181. They asked: "Fool of Love, why do you defend Love when it torments your body and your heart?" He answered: "Because it increases my merits and my happiness."

182. The Lover complained to the Beloved, because He caused Love so grievously to torment him. The Beloved replied by increasing his trials and tears.

183. They said: "Fool of Love, why do you make excuses for the guilty?" He answered: "So I will not be like those who accuse the innocent with the guilty."

184. The Beloved raised the understanding of the Lover so he could grasp His greatness, recall his shortcomings

so he might overcome them, and soar loftily to love the perfections of the Beloved.

185. The Lover sang of his Beloved: "So great is my will to love You that through my love for You the things I once hated are now a greater happiness and joy to me that those I once loved without loving You."

186. The Lover went through a great city and asked if there were any people with whom he might speak about his Beloved. They showed him a poor man who was weeping for love, and who sought a companion with whom to speak of love.

187. The Lover was perplexed because he wondered how his trials could have their source in his Beloved's glory.

188. The Lover's thoughts lay between forgetfulness of his torments and remembrance of his joys; for the joys of love drive the memory of sorrow away, and the tortures of love recall the happiness it brings.

189. They asked the Lover: "Will your Beloved ever take away your love?" He answered: "No, not while memory has the power to remember, or understanding the power to grasp the glory of my Beloved."

190. They said: "Fool of Love, what is the greatest comparison of all that can be made?" He replied: "That of the Lover with the Beloved." "Why?" they asked. He answered: "Because of the love each one has."

191. They asked the Beloved: "Have You never had pity?" He answered: "If I had not had pity, my Lover would have never learned to love Me, nor would I have tormented him with sighs and tears, with trials and with griefs."

192. The Lover was in a vast forest, seeking his Beloved. He came upon Truth and Falsehood arguing about his Beloved, for Truth praised Him and Falsehood accused Him. The Lover cried out to Love to come to the aid of Truth.

193. The Lover was tempted to leave the Beloved so his memory might awaken and find his Beloved's Presence once more. If he did this, he would remember Him more deeply, his understanding would soar higher in comprehending Him, and his will for loving Him would grow stronger.

194. One day the Lover stopped remembering his Beloved, and on the next day he remembered he had forgotten Him. On the day the Lover remembered he had forgotten his Beloved, he was in sorrow and pain for his forgetfulness and in glory and bliss for his remembrance.

195. The Lover wanted so earnestly to praise and honor his Beloved, he doubted if he could remember Him enough; so strongly did he abhor the dishonor paid to his Beloved, he doubted he could abhor it enough. Because of this, the Lover was speechless and perplexed between his love and his fear of the Beloved.

196. The Lover's joys and torments were mingled and united and became one and the same in the Lover's will. For this reason, the Lover felt as if he were living and dying at one and the same time.

197. For just one hour the Lover would have forgotten his Beloved, so his grief would have some rest. But, since such ignorance had already made him suffer, he had

patience and lifted up his understanding and memory in contemplating his Beloved.

198. So great was the Lover's love of his Beloved that he believed all things He revealed to him. So earnestly did he want to understand Him that he tried to understand by unanswerable reasons all that was said of Him. Thus, the love of the Lover lay always between belief and understanding.

199. They asked the Lover: "What is the farthest thing from your heart?" He answered: "Indifference." "Why?" they asked. He said: "Because nearest to my heart is love, which is the opposite of indifference."

200. They asked: "Fool of Love, do you have envy?" He answered: "Yes, whenever I forget the riches of my Beloved."

201. They asked the Lover: "Do you have riches?" "Yes," he replied, "I have love." "Do you have poverty?" "Yes, I have love." "How can this be?" "I am poor," he answered, "because my love is not greater than it is and because it fills so few others with love for my Beloved."

202. They asked the Lover: "Where is your power?" He answered: "In the power of my Beloved." "How do you strive against your enemies?" "With the strength of my Beloved." "In what do you find consolation?" "In the eternal treasures of my Beloved."

203. They said: "Fool of Love, do you love more your Beloved's mercy or His justice?" He answered: "So greatly do I love and fear justice that it is not in my will to love anything more than my Beloved's justice."

204. In the Lover's conscience and will, sins and merits struggled among themselves. His remorse was

increased by justice and remembrance, but in the will of the Beloved mercy and hope increased the certainty of forgiveness. Merits conquered sins and wrongs in the Lover's penitence.

205. The Lover affirmed that all is perfection in his Beloved, and denied that there is any fault at all in Him. Which of the two—his affirmations or his denials—do you think is greater?

206. Once, an eclipse plunged the earth into darkness. The eclipse reminded the Lover that his sins long ago banished the Beloved from his will, and the darkness had banished the light from his understanding. The Beloved uses the light to reveal Himself to His lovers.

207. Love came to the Lover, and the Lover said: "What do you want?" Love replied: "I have come to nurture and direct your life, so that at death you will be able to defeat your mortal enemies."

208. When the Lover forgot his Beloved, Love fell sick. The Lover himself fell sick when he started thinking too much, and his Beloved gave him trials, longings, and grief.

209. The Lover found a person was dying without love. The Lover wept that a person should die without love, for the dishonor it brought to his Beloved. So, he asked: "Why are you dying without love?" He answered: "Because no one will give me knowledge of love, and no one has taught me to be a lover." The Lover sighed and cried: "Devotion, when will you be so great that sins may diminish and that my Beloved may have many fervent lovers who will praise Him and extol His honors?"

210. The Lover tempted Love to see if he would remain in his mind even if he forgot his Beloved. His heart ceased to think and his eyes to weep; his love vanished, and the Lover was perplexed and speechless. He asked everyone if they had seen Love.

211. Love and loving, Lover and Beloved, are so united in the Beloved that they are unity in Essence. Lover and Beloved are distinct entities, which agree without diversity of essence. The Beloved is to be loved above all other objects of affection.

212. They asked: "Fool of Love, why do you have such great love?" He answered: "Because I must bear heavy burdens as I endure a long and perilous journey in search of my Beloved. I cannot accomplish this journey without great love."

213. The Lover prayed and fasted, wept, gave alms, and traveled afar so that the Beloved's Will might inspire love in His subjects to honor His Name.

214. If the Lover's love is not sufficient to move his Beloved to pity and forgiveness, the Beloved's love is sufficient to give grace and blessings to His creatures.

215. They asked the Lover: "How can you be most like the Beloved?" He answered: "By grasping and loving with all my power the Beloved's virtues."

216. They asked the Lover if his Beloved had any deficiency. "Yes," he answered, "of those who will love and praise Him and extol His virtue."

217. The Beloved chastened His Lover's heart. He suffered grief, dishonor, and death so He might regain the love of those lovers He had lost.

218. The Lover met his Beloved and saw He was very

noble, powerful, and worthy of all honor. He exclaimed: "How strange it is that so few people know and love and honor You as You deserve." The Beloved answered: "People have greatly grieved Me, for I created them to know Me, love Me, and honor Me. There is hardly a person who loves Me for My goodness and nobility." When the Lover heard this, he wept bitterly for the dishonor paid his Beloved, and he said: "O Beloved, how greatly You have honored people and given them so much. Why have people thus forgotten You?"

219. The Lover was praising his Beloved, and he said that He had transcended place, because He is in a place where place is not. When they asked the Lover where his Beloved was, he replied: "He is, but no one knows where." Yet he knew the Beloved was in his remembrance.

220. With His merits, the Beloved bought a slave and made him suffer griefs and thoughts, sighs and tears. He asked: "What would you like to eat and drink?" The slave replied: "I will eat and drink whatever You do." "What will you wear?" "I will wear whatever You want me to wear." "Don't you have any self-will?" asked the Beloved. The slave answered: "A subject and a slave has no will other than to obey his Lord and Beloved."

221. The Beloved asked His Lover if he had patience. The Lover replied: "Everything pleases me, so I have no need of patience; for the one who cannot rule his will cannot but be impatient."

222. Love chose the people to whom he gave himself.

Since he gave himself to few and inspired very few with fervent love, the Lover accused him before the Beloved. Love defended himself and said: "I don't strive against free will, for I want my lovers to have great merit and great glory."

223. There was great discord between the Lover and Love, because the Lover was weary with the trials Love made him go through. They argued about whether Love or the Lover was to blame. They asked the Beloved to judge the argument; the Beloved chastened the Lover with griefs and rewarded him with increase of love.

224. There was some question whether Love had more thought than patience. The Lover resolved the question, saying that Love is born in thought and nourished with patience.

225. The Lover has the Beloved's virtues for neighbors; the Beloved's neighbors are the thoughts of His Lover and the trials and tears that he bears for Love's sake.

226. The Lover's will wanted to soar on high so he might greatly love his Beloved. The Lover's will commanded the understanding to soar as high as it could, and the understanding also commanded the memory, so that all three mounted to the contemplation of the Beloved in His honors.

227. The Lover's will left him and gave itself up to the Beloved. The Beloved gave the will to the Lover, so he could love and serve Him.

228. The Lover said: "Do not let my Beloved think I have left Him to love another, for my love has united me to One, and to One Alone." The Beloved answered: "Do not let my Lover think he alone loves and serves

Me, for many lovers loved Me more fervently and longer than he."

229. The Lover said to the Beloved: "You, who are worthy of all love, have taught my eyes to see and my ears to hear of Your honor. These have trained my heart to thoughts which have brought tears to my eyes and griefs to my body." The Beloved answered: "If I hadn't taught and guided you this way, your name would not have been written in the book of eternal blessing."

230. In the Lover's heart are gathered the Beloved's perfections, increasing his thoughts and trials, so he would have died if the Beloved had increased in him the thoughts of His greatness.

231. The Beloved came to stay in the Lover's abode, and the Lover made Him a bed of thoughts, serving Him with sighs and tears. The Beloved compensated him with memories.

232. Love put trials and joys together into the Lover's thoughts, and the joys complained of the arrangement and accused Love before the Beloved. But when He parted the joys from the torments Love gives to his lovers, the torments vanished.

233. The marks of the love the Lover has for his Beloved are tears, tribulations, and death. With these marks the Lover preaches of his Beloved before all the lovers.

234. The Lover went into solitude, and his heart was accompanied by thoughts, his eyes by tears, and his body by afflictions and fasts. When the Lover returned to the companionship of others, though, these things left him, and the Lover remained quite alone in the company of many people.

235. Love is an ocean; its waves are troubled by the winds, and it has no port or shore. The Lover perished in this ocean, and with him his torments perished.

236. They asked: "Fool of Love, what is love?" He answered: "Love is theory and practice working together toward one end, toward which the will of the Lover moves, that people may honor and serve his Beloved." Do you think that the Lover's will conforms to this end when he longs to be with his Beloved?

237. They asked the Lover: "Who is the Beloved?" He answered: "He is the One who makes me love, desire, faint, sigh, weep, endure reproaches, suffer, and die."

238. They asked the Beloved: "Who is Your Lover?" He answered: "The one who fears nothing so he may honor and praise My Name, and renounces all things to obey My commandments and advice."

239. They said: "Fool of Love, are the trials of love or the trials of those who don't love the heavier and more grievous?" He anwered: "Ask that question to those that do penance for the love of their Beloved and of those that do penance from fear of the pains of hell."

240. The Lover slept, and Love died, for he had nowhere to live. The Lover woke up, and Love revived in the thoughts the Lover sent to his Beloved.

241. The Lover said: "Infused knowledge comes from the will, devotion, and prayer; acquired knowledge comes from study and understanding." Which of these, do you think, is more proper and pleasing to the Lover, and which does he possess more perfectly?

242. They asked the Lover: "From where do your needs come?" He replied: "From thoughts, longing, adoration, trials, perseverance." "And from where do all

these things come?" "From love." "And from where does love come?" "From my Beloved." "And from where does your Beloved come?" "From Himself alone."

243. They said: "Fool of Love, will you be free of all things?" He answered: Yes, except of my Beloved." "Will you be a prisoner?" "Yes, of sighs and thoughts, trials, perils, exiles, tears, so I may serve my Beloved, who created me to praise Him."

244. Love tormented the Lover, and he wept and complained. His Beloved called him to come to Him and be healed. The nearer the Lover came to the Beloved, the more love tormented him, for he felt greater love. The more he felt love, the greater was his joy, and the more perfectly did the Beloved heal him of his troubles.

245. Love became sick, and the Lover tended him with patience, perseverance, obedience, and hope. Love got well, and the Lover became sick. He was healed by the Beloved, Who made him remember His virtues and His honors.

246. They said: "Fool of Love, what is solitude?" He answered: "It is solace and companionship between Lover and Beloved." "What are solace and companionship?" "Solitude in the Lover's heart when he remembers nothing except his Beloved."

247. They asked the Lover: "Is there greater peril in trials endured for love's sake or in pleasure?" The Lover spoke with his Beloved and answered: "The perils that come through afflictions are the perils of impatience; those that come through pleasures are the perils of ignorance."

248. The Beloved gave Love his freedom and allowed people to take him to themselves as much as they would, but few would take Love. Because of this the Lover wept and was sad at the dishonor paid to Love in this world by the ungrateful and by false lovers.

249. Love destroyed all that was in his faithful Lover's heart, and the Lover would have died if had not possessed the remembrance of the Beloved.

250. The Lover had two thoughts: one, of his Beloved's Essence and Virtues, and the other, of his Beloved's works. Which of these thoughts, do you think, was more excellent and pleasing to the Beloved?

251. The Lover died, because of his great love. The Beloved buried him, and the Lover rose again. Do you think the Lover received the greater blessing from his death or his resurrection?

252. In the Beloved's prison-house were evils, perils, griefs, and trials, so that the Lover would not be prevented from praising the Beloved's honors and filling with love those that hold Him in contempt.

253. One day the Lover was in the presence of many people whom his Beloved had too greatly honored in this world, because they dishonored Him in their thoughts. These people despised the Beloved and mocked His servants. The Lover wept and cried in a loud voice: "Did anyone ever commit so great a sin as despising my Beloved?"

254. They said: "Fool of Love, would you be willing to die?" He answered: "Yes, to the pleasures of this world and the thoughts of the unhappy sinners who forget and dishonor my Beloved."

255. "If you speak the truth, Fool of Love, you will be beaten, mocked, tormented, and killed." He answered: "From these words it follows that if I speak falsehoods I should be praised, loved, served, and honored by other people, and cast out by lovers of my Beloved."

256. One day false flatterers were speaking ill of the Lover in his Beloved's presence. The Lover was patient, and the Beloved showed His justice, wisdom, and power. The Lover preferred to be reproved in this way rather than to be one who falsely accused him.

257. The Beloved planted many seeds in His Lover's heart, but only one of them took life and bore flowers and fruit. Will there come many seeds from this one fruit?

258. The Beloved is far above Love, and the Lover is far beneath it. Love lies between them and makes the Beloved descend to the Lover and the Lover ascend to the Beloved. This ascending and descending are the beginning and the life of that love where the Lover suffers and the Beloved is served.

259. The Beloved stands on the right side of Love, and the Lover stands on the left side of Love. Thus, the Lover cannot reach the Beloved unless he passes through Love.

260. The Beloved stands in front of Love, and beyond the Beloved stands the Lover. The Lover cannot reach Love unless his thoughts and desires have first passed through the Beloved.

261. The Beloved made Two like Himself for the Lover to love equally in honor and valor. The Lover loved all Three equally, even though love is one only in

significance of the essential unity of One in Three.

262. The Beloved clothed Himself in the dress of His Lover, so he could be His companion in glory forever. The Lover wanted to wear crimson garments daily so his clothes would be like the Beloved's.

263. They asked the Lover: "What did your Beloved do before the creation of the world?" He answered: "My Beloved was, because of His Nature, eternal, personal, and infinite."

264. The Lover wept when he saw the unbelievers losing his Beloved through ignorance, but he rejoiced in his Beloved's justice, which punishes those who know Him and are disobedient to Him. Do you think the Lover's sorrow or his joy was greater? Was his joy greater when he saw his Beloved honored than his sorrow at seeing Him despised?

265. The Lover contemplated his Beloved in the greatest diversity and harmony of virtues and in His Being and perfection, which have greater harmony between themselves than nonexistence and perfection.

266. The diversity and harmony the Lover found in the Beloved revealed to him His plurality and unity.

267. They said to the Lover: "If corruption, which is opposed to nonexistence, were eternally corrupting, it would be impossible for nonexistence to be in harmony with corruption or anything that is corrupted." From these words the Lover saw eternal generation in his Beloved.

268. If the Lover's love for his Beloved were based on falseness, whatever diminished this love would be truth. If this were so, it would follow that there would be a

lack of greatness and truth in the Beloved, and that He would be in harmony with the false.

269. The Lover praised his Beloved and said that if He possessed the greatest degree of perfection and the greatest possible freedom from imperfection, his Beloved must be simple and pure actuality in essence and in His works. While the Lover praised his Beloved, the Beloved revealed His Trinity to him.

270. The Lover found great harmony in the numbers 1 and 3, because by these numbers every bodily form passes from nonexistence to existence. By considering this harmony of number, the Lover was able to contemplate the Unity and the Trinity of his Beloved.

271. The Lover praised his Beloved's power, wisdom, and will, for his Beloved created all things except sin. And yet, sin would not have existed except for His power, wisdom, and will. But neither the Beloved's power, wisdom, nor will are an occasion of sin.

272. The Lover praised and loved his Beloved, for He had created him and given him all things. He praised and loved Him, too, because the Beloved took the Lover's form and nature. And you could ask: "Which praise and which love was more perfect?"

273. Love tempted the Lover and asked him whether the Beloved showed the greater love in taking the Lover's nature or in redeeming him. The Lover was perplexed, but eventually replied that Redemption was necessary to put away unhappiness and the Incarnation was necessary to bestow happiness. This reply raised the question again: "In which act was the greater love?"

274. The Lover went from door to door asking alms to keep in mind his Beloved's love for his servants and to practice humility, poverty, and patience, all virtues pleasing to his Beloved.

275. They asked the Lover's forgiveness, in the name of his Beloved's love. The Lover not only forgave them but also gave them himself and his possessions.

276. With tears in his eyes, the Lover described the Passion and the pains that his Beloved bore for his love. With sadness and heavy thoughts, he wrote down the words he had spoken, and mercy and hope comforted him.

277. Love and the Beloved came to see the Lover, who was sleeping. The Beloved cried out to His Lover, and Love woke him up. The Lover obeyed Love and answered his Beloved.

278. The Beloved taught His Lover how to love, and Love taught him how to endure trials. Patience taught the Lover how to bear the afflictions he would suffer for the love of the Beloved.

279. The Beloved asked people if they had seen His Lover, and they asked Him: "What are Your Lover's qualities?" The Beloved said: "My Lover is ardent yet fearful, rich and yet poor, joyful, sad, and pensive, and every day he grieves because of his love."

280. They asked the Lover: "Will you sell your desire?" He answered: "I have already sold it to my Beloved, for a price so great it would buy the whole world."

281. They said: "Preach, Fool of Love, and speak about your Beloved; weep and fast." The Lover renounced the world and went out seeking his Beloved, praising

Him in those places where He was dishonored.

282. The Lover built a beautiful city where his Beloved could live. He built the city with love, thoughts, tears, complaints, and griefs; he adorned the city with joy, hope, and devotion; and he furnished the city with faith, justice, prudence, and strength.

283. The Lover drank at the Beloved's fountain. There the Beloved washed the Lover's feet, even though many times he had forgotten and despised His honors, and the world suffered because of his forgetfulness.

284. They said: "Fool of Love, what is sin?" He answered: "Sin is intention directed and turned away from Intention and Reason."

285. The Lover realized that the world is a thing created, since eternity is more in harmony with his Beloved than with the world, a finite quantity. Thus, in the Beloved's justice the Lover realized that the Beloved's eternity must have been before time and finite quantities.

286. The Lover defended his Beloved against those who said the world is eternal. He argued that his Beloved's justice would not be perfect if He did not restore every soul to its own body, and He could not perform such acts in a material order. If the world were eternal, it could not be directed to one goal; yet, if it were not so directed, the Beloved would be lacking in perfection of wisdom and will.

287. They said: "Fool of Love, How do you know that the Catholic faith is true, and that the beliefs of other religions are false and erroneous?" He answered: "In the ten conditions of the *Book of the Gentiles and the Three Wise Men.*"

288. They asked: "Fool of Love, what is the beginning of wisdom?" He answered: "In faith and devotion, which are ladders the understanding can use to comprehend the Beloved's secrets." "Where do faith and devotion begin?" He replied: "In my Beloved, who illumines faith and kindles devotion."

289. They asked the Lover: "What is greater: the possible or the impossible?" He answered: "The possible is greater in the creature, and the impossible in my Beloved."

290. They said: "Fool of Love, which is greater: difference or harmony?" He answered: "Except in my Beloved, difference is greater in plurality and harmony in unity. In my Beloved they are equal in difference and in unity."

291. They asked the Lover: "What is valor?" He answered: "It is the opposite of what the world calls valor and which false and vain lovers desire."

292. They said: "Fool of Love, have you seen one without his reason?" He answered: "I have seen a Bishop who had many cups on his table, many silver plates and knives, and great wealth in his vaults, but few poor people at the gates of his palace."

293. They said: "Fool of Love, do you know what evil is?" He answered: "Evil thoughts." "And what is loyalty?" "It is fear of my Beloved, born of love and shame." "And what is honor?" He replied: "It is to think upon my Beloved, to desire Him, and to praise His honors."

294. Because he was tired of the trials and tribulations he suffered for love's sake, the Lover became impatient. The Beloved admonished him, saying that the one affected by either trouble or happiness knew little of

love. Weeping and sorrowful, the Lover begged his Beloved to restore his love.

295. They said: "Fool of Love, what is love?" He answered: "Love throws the free into bondage and frees those who are in bondage. Who can say whether love is nearer to freedom or bondage?"

296. The Beloved called His Lover. The Lover answered: "What would You like, my Beloved, Who are the sight of my eyes, thought of my thought, love of my love, fullness of my perfections, and the source of my beginnings?"

297. "My Beloved," said the Lover, "I come to You, and walk in You, for You call me. I discover my contemplation in contemplating Your contemplation. I take my virtue from Your virtue. I greet You with Your greeting which is my greeting in Yours, and I hope for Your eternal blessing where I am blessed in my blessing."

298. "You are so highly exalted, my Beloved, that my will is raised up."

299. "My Beloved, You are the glory of my glory. With Your glory and in Your glory do You give glory to my glory. By Your glory both trials and griefs are equally glorious to me, for they come to honor Your glory with the joys and thoughts that Your glory brings me."

300. "My Beloved, You hold me enthralled with Your love, for You are nothing else except love, and You make me to be alone with Your Love and Honors for my only company. Your uniqueness in virtues makes me praise and honor its valor without fearing those who do not know You and do not have You alone in their love."

301. "My Beloved, You are solace of all solace. Your solace provides comfort for my griefs and tribulations."

302. The Lover complained to his Lord about his Beloved and his Beloved about his Lord. The Lord and the Beloved said: "Who is this that divides Us, that are One only?" The Lover answered: "It is pity, which belongs to the Lord, and tribulation, which comes through the Beloved."

303. The Lover was in peril in the great ocean of love, and he trusted in his Beloved, Who brought him troubles, thoughts, tears, sighs, and griefs because the ocean was of love and honor due to His honors.

304. The Lover rejoiced in the Beloved's Being, for, he said, "from His Being all other Being comes. He sustains all other Being, and all other Being is bound to honor and serve my Beloved's Being. By no being can he be condemned or destroyed, or made less or greater." "What is the Being of Your Beloved?" they asked. He answered: "Like the sun that shines all over the world, His Being is a bright ray throughout all things. When the sun withdraws its brightness, it leaves all things in darkness, but when it shines forth, it brings the day. Even more so is my Beloved."

305. "My Beloved, in Your greatness do You make my desires, thought and afflictions great, for You are so great that all things that have remembrance and understanding and joy of You are great. Your greatness makes all things contrary to Your commandments and honors small."

306. "In Eternity my Beloved has beginning, had beginning, and will have beginning, and in Eternity He

has no beginning, neither has had nor will have beginning. These beginnings are no contradictions in my Beloved, because He is eternal and has in Himself Unity and Trinity."

307. "My Beloved is one, and in His unity my thought and my love are united in one will. My Beloved's unity is the source of unities and pluralities. My Beloved's plurality is the source of all pluralities and unities."

308. "Sovereign Good is my Beloved's good, Who is the Good of my good. For my Beloved is Good without other good, for if He were not, my good would be from another Sovereign Good. Since this is not so, let all my good honor the Sovereign Good."

309. "My Beloved, You know my sinfulness. Be merciful, and forgive me. Your knowledge is greater than mine, yet even I know Your forgiveness and love. For You have given me contrition and grief and the desire to suffer death so Your name may be exalted."

310. "My Beloved, Your power can save me through Your goodness, mercy and forgiveness, but it can condemn me through Your justice and my failures and imperfections. Let Your power be perfected in me, whether it brings salvation or punishment."

311. "My Beloved, Truth visits my sorrowful heart and makes me weep wherever my will loves Truth. Since Your Truth, my Beloved, is sovereign, it raises up my will so it may honor You and hate my sins."

312. "Never was anything true that was not in my Beloved, and all that is false is not in my Beloved. All that will be, or was, or is, must be true if my Beloved is in it."

313. The Beloved created, and the Lover destroyed. The Beloved judged, and the Lover wept. Then the Beloved redeemed him, and the Lover again had glory. The Beloved finished his work, and the Lover remained forever in his Beloved's companionship.

314. On the paths of feeling, imagination, understanding, and will, the Lover searched for his Beloved. On those paths the Lover endured perils and griefs for his Beloved's sake, so he might raise his will and understanding to the Beloved. For the Beloved wills that His lovers may comprehend and love Him deeply.

315. The Beloved's perfection moved His Lover to be, and the Lover's shortcomings moved him to be no more. Which of these forces, do you think, has the greater power over the Lover?

316. "You have placed me, my Beloved, between my evil and Your good. In Your patience and humility, may You have pity and mercy on me, and restore, forgive, and help me. I am sorrowful and repentant, and I will persevere with sighs and tears for Your Passion."

317. "My Beloved, You make me to love. If You do not give me help in loving, why did You create me? Why did You endure such grief for my sake and bear upon Yourself so grievous a Passion? Since You did help me to rise, Beloved, help me descend to remembrance and hatred of my sins, so my thoughts may rise again to honor and praise You."

318. "My Beloved, You have made my will free to honor or despise Your valor, so in my will my love to You may be increased."

319. "In giving me such freedom, my Beloved, You have

put my will in danger. Remember Your Lover who places his free will in Your service, praises Your honor, and increases grief and tears in his body."

320. "My Beloved, neither fault nor sin came to Your Lover from You, nor can Your Lover attain perfection except through Your grace and forgiveness. Remember the Lover in his trials and tribulations."

321. "My Beloved, Who in one Name, Jesus Christ, are named both God and Man, by that Name I adore You as God and Man."

322. The Lover wept and said: "Beloved, You were always liberal to Your Lover in giving him being, redeeming him, and in granting him many creatures to serve him. Why, then, Beloved, should you spare Your Lover tears, thoughts, griefs, wisdom, and love that he may honor Your name? Beloved, the Lover asks for long life, so that he may receive many of these gifts."

323. "My Beloved, if You help just people against their enemies, help me increase my thoughts and desires for Your honor. If You help sinners lead just lives, help Your Lover sacrifice his will to Your praise, and his body for a testimony of love."

324. "My Beloved makes no distinction between humility, the humble, and the humbled, for all these are humility in pure essence." The Lover reproves Pride, for the Lover wants to raise to his Beloved the ones He has greatly honored in this world, but whom Pride has clothed with hypocrisy, vanity, and vanities."

325. Humility has humbled the Beloved to the depths of

the Lover, through the Lover's contrition and devotion. In which of these two manners has the Beloved humbled Himself more?

326. Because of His perfect love and His Lover's needs, the Beloved had mercy on His Lover. Which of these two reasons, do you think, moved the Beloved to forgive the sins of His Lover?

327. Our Lady and the angels and saints in glory prayed to my Beloved. When she remembered the errors of this world, she remembered the great justice of my Beloved, and the great ignorance of His lovers.

328. The Lover lifted up the powers of his soul, and climbed the ladder of humanity to glory in the Divine Nature. By the Divine Nature the powers of his soul descended to glory in the human nature of his Beloved.

329. The straighter the paths by which the Lover journeys to his Beloved, the vaster is his love, and the straighter the paths, the broader are the paths. In these ways the Lover receives love, trials and griefs, joys and consolations, from his Beloved.

330. Love comes from love, thoughts come from griefs, and tears come from griefs. Love leads to love as thoughts lead to tears and griefs to sighs. The Beloved watches His Lover, who bears all these afflictions for His love.

331. The Lover's desires and his memories of the Beloved's nobility kept vigils and traveled on pilgrimages. They brought the Lover graces that illumined his understanding with splendor and increased his love.

332. Using his imagination, the Lover pictured the bodily

features of his Beloved's Face. Using his understanding, he blessed this Face in spiritual things, and using his will, he worshiped his Beloved's Face in all creatures.

333. The Lover purchased a day of tears with another day of thoughts, and he sold a day of love for a day of tribulation. Both his thoughts and love increased.

334. The Lover was in another country, and he forgot his Beloved. He missed his wife, his children, and his friends. But he remembered his Beloved so he would be comforted and so his exile would not cause him yearning or sorrow.

335. The Lover heard the Beloved's words, and his understanding grasped Him in His words. The Lover's will took pleasure in what he heard, and his memory recalled the Beloved's virtues and promises.

336. The Lover heard people speaking evil of his Beloved, and his understanding grasped the Beloved's justice and patience. His justice would punish the evil speakers, while His patience would await their sorrow and repentance. In which of these two, do you think, did the Lover believe more earnestly?

337. The Lover became sick, and he wrote his will with the Beloved's advice. He bequeathed his sins and faults to contrition and penance, worldly pleasures to contempt. To his eyes he left tears, to his heart sighs and love, to his understanding the graces of his Beloved, and to his memory the Passion that his Beloved endured for his sake. To his activity he bequeathed the guidance of unbelievers, who go to their doom through ignorance.

338. The scent of flowers brought the evil stench of riches

and meanness, of ignorance and pride, to the Lover's mind. The taste of sweet things made him think of the bitterness of worldly possessions and of entering and quitting this world. The enjoyment of earthly pleasures made him feel how quickly this world passes, and how the delights that are here so pleasant are the occasion of eternal torments.

339. The Lover endured hunger and thirst, heat and cold, poverty and nakedness, sickness and tribulation. He would have died if he had not remembered his Beloved, Who healed him with hope and memory, with the renunciation of the world, and contempt for other people's ridiculings of him.

340. The Lover made his bed between trials and joys. He lay down to sleep in joys and woke up in trials. Which of these two do you think is more proper to the Lover's bed?

341. The Lover lay down to sleep in anger, for he feared the ridicule of people. He woke up in patience, remembering the praises of his Beloved. Do you think the Lover was more ashamed of his Beloved or of other people?

342. The Lover reflected upon death, and he was afraid until he remembered his Beloved's city, to which love and death are the gates and the entrance.

343. The Lover complained to his Beloved about the daily temptations that afflicted his thoughts. The Beloved replied and said that temptations are an occasion where one remembers God and loves His honors and perfection.

344. The Lover was distressed about losing a greatly prized

jewel, until his Beloved asked him: "Which thing is more profitable, your lost jewel or your patience in all your Beloved's works?"

345. The Lover fell asleep thinking about the trials and hindrances he met in serving his Beloved, and he was afraid his works might be lost through such hindrances. But the Beloved sent him consciousness, and the Lover woke up to his Beloved's merits and powers.

346. The Lover made long journeys over rough roads, carrying the heavy burden that Love makes his lovers bear. The Lover unburdened his soul of the cares and pleasures of this world so his body could bear the weight more easily, and his soul could journey along these roads in his Beloved's company.

347. One day, others spoke ill of the Beloved in front of the Lover. But the Lover did not reply or defend his Beloved. Who was more to be blamed, those who spoke ill of the Beloved or the Lover, who was silent and did not defend Him?

348. As the Lover contemplated his Beloved, his understanding grasped subtleties, and his will was kindled with love. In which of these two, do you think, did his memory grow more fruitful in thinking about his Beloved?

349. With fervor and fear the Lover journeyed to honor his Beloved. Fervor carried him along, and fear protected him from danger. While he was journeying, the Lover found sighs and tears, which brought him greetings from his Beloved. Through which of these four companions do you think the Lover received the greatest consolation in his Beloved?

350. The Lover gazed upon himself so he might be a mirror in which he might see his Beloved. He gazed upon his Beloved like a mirror in which he might know himself. Which of these mirrors, do you think, was nearer to his understanding?

351. When he met Theology and Philosophy, Medicine and Law, the Lover asked them if they had seen his Beloved. The first wept, the second was doubtful, and the other two were glad. What do you think each of these happenings meant to the Lover?

352. Full of tears and anguish, the Lover went searching for his Beloved by the paths of the senses and by intellectual roads. Which of these roads, do you think, did the Lover follow first? On which of these roads did the Beloved reveal Himself more openly?

353. At the Day of Judgment the Beloved will place all that people have given Him in this world on one side, and He will place all that they have given to the world on the other side. Thus it will be seen clearly how much they have loved Him and which of their two gifts is the greater and nobler.

354. When the Lover's will was enamored of itself, his understanding asked: "Is it more like the Beloved to love oneself or to love the Beloved? The Beloved is worthier of love than anything else." How do you think the will could reply most truly to the understanding?

355. They said: "Fool of Love, what is the greatest and noblest love to be found in the creature?" He answered: "That which is one with the Creator." "Why?" "Because there is nothing with which the Creator can make a nobler creature."

356. One day the Lover was praying, and he realized he was not weeping. So that he might weep, he turned his thoughts to wealth, women, and vanity. His understanding found that people serve these worldly things more than they serve his Beloved, and he began weeping and his soul was in sorrow and pain.

357. As the Lover was walking, contemplating his Beloved, he met many people who asked him for news. The Lover, who was rejoicing in his Beloved, did not give them what they asked, because he would have to leave the companionship of his Beloved to answer their questions.

358. Within and without the Lover was covered with love, and he went seeking his Beloved. Love said to the Lover: "Where are you going?" He answered: "I am going to my Beloved so you will be increased."

359. They said: "Fool of Love, what is Religion?" He aswered: "Purity of thought, longing for death so the Beloved might be honored, and renouncing the world so that nothing may hinder one from contemplating Him and speaking truth about His honors."

360. They said: "Fool of Love, what are trials, sighs, tears, afflictions, and perils in a Lover?" He answered: "The joys of the Beloved." "Why is this so?" "So the Beloved may be loved more deeply and the Lover rewarded more richly."

361. They asked the Lover: "Where is love the greater, in the Lover that lives or in the Lover that dies?" He replied: "In the Lover that dies." "Why?" "Because in one that lives love may yet be greater, but in one that dies it can be no greater."

362. Two lovers met; the one revealed his Beloved, and the other grasped Him. They argued about which of the two was nearer his Beloved, and in the solution the Lover grasped the demonstration of the Trinity.

363. They said: "Fool of Love, why do you speak with such subtlety?" He answered: "So I may lift my understanding to the heights of my Beloved's nobility and so more people will honor, love, and serve Him."

364. The Lover drank deeply of the wine of memory, understanding, and love for the Beloved. The Beloved made the wine bitter with His tears and with the weeping of His Lover.

365. Love inflamed the Lover with remembrance of his Beloved. The Beloved cooled his ardor with weeping and tears and forgetfulness of the delights of this world. So his love grew when he remembered for Whom he suffered griefs and afflictions, and for Whom the people of the world bore trials and persecutions.

366. They said: "Fool of Love, what is this world?" He answered: "It is the prison-house of those who love and serve my Beloved." "Who is the one who imprisons them?" He replied: "Conscience, love, fear, renunciation and contrition, and the companionship of willful people, and the labor that knows no rewards."

Because Blanquerna wanted to write *The Art of Contemplation,* he ended *The Book of the Lover and the Beloved,* which is now ended, to the glory and praise of our Lord God.

THE ART OF
CONTEMPLATION

Prologue

1. Our Sovereign Good is so high and excellent, and people are so low because of guilt and sins, that a hermit or holy person is greatly hindered in lifting up his soul to contemplate God. Since an art of contemplation is of great help, Blanquerna the hermit considered how he might write an Art of Contemplation that should help him have devotion in his heart, and weeping and tears in his eyes, and enable his will and understanding to rise to the contemplation of God in His honors and His wonders.

2. After much reflection, Blanquerna the hermit wrote a Book of Contemplation, which he divided into twelve parts: Divine Virtues, Essences, Unity, Trinity, Incarnation, *Pater Noster, Ave Maria,* Commandments, *Miserere mei Deus,* Sacraments, Virtues, Vices.

3. The art of this book is that the Divine Virtues should first be contemplated in relation to each other, and they should then be contemplated with the other parts of the book. The contemplative's soul should be focused on the Divine virtues in his memory, understanding, and will. He should learn also to unite in his soul the Divine Virtues and the other parts of this book to the glory and honor of the Divine Virtues, which are these: Goodness, Greatness, Eternity, Power, Wisdom, Love, Virtue, Truth, Glory, Perfection, Justice, Liberality, Mercy, Humility, Dominion, Patience.

4.   These virtues may be contemplated in various ways. One way is to contemplate one with another, or one with two or more.

      A second way is to contemplate these virtues in relation to Essence, Unity, Trinity, or Incarnation, and so with the other parts of this book. A third way is to contemplate Essence, Unity, Trinity, or Incarnation with these virtues.

      Yet another way is in the words of the *Pater Noster* and the *Ave Maria*. A person may contemplate God or His works with all sixteen virtues or with any of them, depending on whether the contemplation is long or short and as the art of contemplation fits certain virtues rather than others.

5.   The conditions of the art are that a person should be suitably disposed toward contemplation and in an appropriate place, for a place that is bustling and noisy might hinder one's contemplation. The chief condition is that a person entering contemplation not be hindered by worldly cares in his memory, understanding, or will.

CHAPTER ONE

How Blanquerna Contemplated the Virtues of God

1. Blanquerna rose at midnight and gazed upon the heavens and the stars, casting everything out of his mind, and fixing his thoughts upon the virtues of God. He was eager to contemplate the goodness of God in all the sixteen virtues and the sixteen virtues in the goodness of God. So, falling on his knees and raising his hands to the heavens and his thoughts to God, he spoke these words and pondered them in his soul with all the powers of his memory, understanding, and will:

2. "O Sovereign Good, You who are infinitely great in eternity, power, wisdom, love, virtue, truth, glory, perfection, justice, liberality, mercy, humility, dominion, patience: I adore You as I remember, comprehend, love, and speak of You and of all these virtues, which are one with You, as You are one with them, one very Essence without any difference."

3. "O Sovereign Good, who are so great, Sovereign Greatness, who are so good: If You were not eternal, You would not be so great a good that my soul could fill its memory with remembrance of You, nor its understanding with understanding of You, nor its will with love of You. But, since You are infinite and eternal Good, You can fill my whole soul with grace and blessing, so memory, understanding, and love

may be given to You, O infinite and eternal Sovereign Good."

4.   Through the power Blanquerna remembered in Sovereign Goodness, he gained power and strength to contemplate a greatness so exceedingly great that it had the infinite power of movement. As Blanquerna reflected on this greatness, he marvelled even more when to this goodness he joined eternity, which has neither beginning nor end. While Blanquerna was absorbed in this reflection, he remembered how great a good is Divine power, which can be so great and so everlasting, and whose knowledge and will are infinite and eternal, as are its virtue, truth, glory, perfection, justice, liberality, mercy, humility, dominion, and patience.

5.   As Blanquerna pursued his contemplation in this way, his heart began to burn within him, and his eyes to weep, at the great joy he had in remembering, understanding, and loving such noble virtues in Sovereign Goodness. But before he could perfectly weep, he fell to thinking and doubting how it could be that, before the creation of the world, God should have justice, liberality, mercy, humility, and dominion. Through the alliance of understanding and imagination, doubt chilled the warmth of his heart. So Blanquerna parted the two, and exalted understanding, remembering how the Sovereign Good is infinite in all perfection and through His own virtue and glory, He may have and can have to so great a degree of perfection all the virtues before the creation of the world and after the creation of the world.

Before the creation of the world, though, there was no person who might receive the grace and influence of the Sovereign Good's virtues.

6. Blanquerna's will was now joyful because his understanding had now comprehended God's infinite power, which in justice, liberality, and the like must have been before the world's creation. If this were not so, it would follow that greatness, power, eternity, and virtue were lacking in Sovereign Goodness. Since it is impossible that God lacks anything, the will set Blanquerna's heart so fiercely on fire that his eyes were abundantly filled with tears.

7. While Blanquerna contemplated and wept, his memory, understanding, and will talked together and were delighted in God's virtues. "Memory," said Understanding, "what do you remember of God's goodness, wisdom, and love. And You, O Will, what do you love in them?" Memory answered: "When I consider how great a good it is to know oneself to be greater and nobler in knowledge and will than any other creature, I feel not so high nor so great as when I remember the Sovereign Good, Who is infinite in knowledge and will. And I feel exalted when I consider eternity, power, virtue, truth, and the rest." With these words and many others, Memory replied to Understanding. Will answered in much the same manner, saying she felt not so great or high when she loved the Sovereign Good because He is more loving and wise than any other, as when she loved Him because of His infinite and eternal wisdom and love. After these words, Understanding said to Memory

and Will that her own state was much like theirs in the contemplation of the Sovereign Good.

8. Memory, Understanding, and Will agreed that they would contemplate the Sovereign Good in His virtue, truth, and glory. Memory recalled the virtue of the infinite Good, His virtue being infinite in truth and glory. Understanding grasped what Memory recalled, and Will loved what Memory recalled and Understanding grasped. Once again Memory turned to remembrance and recalled the infinite truth of Sovereign Good, which possesses virtue and glory. Understanding grasped infinite glory and our glorious Sovereign Good, and Will loved this wholly and in the unity of one actuality, in one and the same perfection.

9. Blanquerna asked of his Understanding: "If the Sovereign Good gives me salvation, what will you grasp?" Understanding answered: "I shall grasp the mercy, humility, and liberality of God." "And You, Memory, if He condemn me, what will you remember?" He answered: "I shall remember God's justice, dominion, perfection, and power." "And You, Will, what will you love?" He answered: "I will love what Memory recalls, for the Sovereign Good's virtues are worthy in themselves to be loved."

10. After these words, Blanquerna remembered his sins and realized how great a good it is that God has patience.

   He asked the Will: "What thanks shall I give to God's patience that has put up with me?" Will answered and said that he should love justice in his Sovereign Good, even if his Understanding knew that he would be punished by damnation for his sins. Blanquerna was very pleased with Will's answer, and he praised and blessed patience in the Sovereign Good through all the Divine virtues.

11. In this way Blanquerna contemplated the Divine virtues, and he gave thanks to God because He had humbled him by guiding him in his contemplation. As he was about to cease his contemplation, he realized that he had not contemplated God's patience as highly as he had contemplated the other virtues. So he turned again to contemplation and said he adored and contemplated God's patience since it was one and the same thing with Sovereign Goodness and with all the other virtues, without any difference.

Understanding marvelled that patience was one thing in essence with the other virtues. But Memory recalled that in God the virtues have no diversity from one another, but, since their operations in the creatures are diverse, they appear diverse.

CHAPTER TWO

How Blanquerna Contemplated by Three and Three the Virtues of God

1. "Divine Goodness," said Blanquerna, "You are of infinite greatness in eternity, You are the good from which all good springs; all good things great and small come from Your great good, and all living things come from Your eternity. Because You are goodness and greatness, I adore You, call upon You, and love You above all that I can understand and remember. I pray that the good You have given me will stay with me, so I will be able to praise and serve You."

2. "Eternal Greatness in power, You are far greater than I can remember or comprehend or love. I lift my power to You so You may make it great and abiding and so I may remember, comprehend, and love Your power, which is infinite and eternal, and from the influence of which I trust will fall grace and blessing."

3. "Eternity, You that have the power of knowledge without end or beginning, You have given me a beginning and created me so I may abide without end. You have the power to save or to damn me. What You will do with me and others, You know eternally, and Your power can accomplish. In Your eternity is no movement or change. I have no power

to know how You will judge me. May it please You, then, that whatever You will do with me, my power and knowledge in this world may be to Your glory and to the praise of Your honor."

4. "Power, that has all knowledge and will in itself; Knowledge, that has all power and will in itself; Will, that has all power and knowledge in itself: Take all my knowledge and power—for You have taken my will already—that they may love and serve You. You, O Power, can know and will, since You are without change. You, O Knowledge, know even as You will. You, O Will, do will even as you will in will, power, and knowledge. Since this is the case, may grace come to my power, knowledge, and will to honor Your power, to my knowledge to honor Your knowledge, and to my will to honor Your love."

5. "Wisdom Divine, in You are virtue and love. You know Yourself to be love above all other love, virtue above all other virtue, and wisdom greater than all other wisdom. If my knowledge grasps that my will has small virtue in loving Your will, Your knowledge must know that Your love is greater in loving me than my love is in loving You. If You did not know this, Your knowledge could not know how much greater virtue there is in Your love and will than in mine, nor could my knowledge and will have the virtue to contemplate God in perfection." While Blanquerna was contemplating, he realized that if God knew that His will loved sin, He would have no virtue with which to love Himself. Thus Blanquerna understood that if he ceased to love God, he would have no ability to cease

to love sin. So Blanquerna wept abundantly when he remembered his sin and guilt.

6. "Love Divine, Your virtue is more real than any love, and Your Truth is more real than all truth. If the sun's virtue is real in giving light, and the fire's virtue is giving warmth, far more real is Your virtue in loving. Between Your love and virtue and truth there is no essential difference, and everything Your love does in truth, it does with infinite virtue in love and truth. Since this is so, I bind myself and all my life to You, O love, O virtue, O truth, so I may honor Your graces and proclaim the truth of Your virtue and Your truth and Your love to all unbelievers and to Christians who have lost their devotion."

7. When he contemplated the Beloved, Virtue, Truth, and Glory met in Blanquerna's thoughts. He considered to which of these he would give the greatest honor in his thoughts and will, but since he could conceive no difference in them, he gave them equal honor in remembering, comprehending, and desiring his Beloved. He said: "I adore You, O Virtue, that have created me; I adore You, O Truth, that will judge me; I adore You, O Glory, where I hope to be glorified in Virtue and Truth."

8. Blanquerna asked of his Beloved's Truth: "What would You be if You weren't glorious and perfect?" Understanding answered Blanquerna: "What but falsehood, or a truth like yours, or nothing at all, or everlasting affliction." Blanquerna said: "If there were no truth, what would glory be?" Memory answered: "Glory would be nonexistent." "And if there were no

perfection, what would glory be?" "It would be nothingness."

9. Blanquerna began contemplating color and grasped the difference between white and black. He considered the glory, perfection, and justice of his Beloved, and he could not find any differences in his Beloved's virtues. He considered glory, and he grasped perfection and justice. He considered perfection, and he grasped justice and glory. He considered justice, and he grasped glory and perfection. Blanquerna marvelled as he considered these things, and he lifted up his memory and understanding and will to the contemplation of the Beloved. He desired His glory, and his eyes were filled with tears. He wept, for he feared the justice of his Beloved.

10. Memory, Understanding, and Will strove to soar to the Beloved. Memory desired to reflect upon perfection; Understanding wanted to contemplate justice; and Will strove to love liberality. None of these three powers could rise above any other, for each needed the Beloved's three virtues, indicating that the Beloved's three virtues are one and the same.

11. "Justice," asked Blanquerna, "what do you desire in my will?" Answering for Justice, Memory said: "I desire contrition and fear; I desire tears in your eyes, sighs in your heart, and afflictions in your body." "And you, Liberality, what do you desire in my will?" Answering for Liberality, Understanding said: "I desire to possess it wholly, for love, for repentance, and for the despising of the world's vanities." "And you, Mercy, what do you desire of my memory and

understanding?" Answering for Mercy, Will said: "I desire your memory wholly, for the remembrance of Mercy's gifts and her forgiveness, and your understanding wholly for comprehension." So Blanquerna gave himself entirely to what his Beloved's virtues desired of him.

12. Blanquerna adored and contemplated liberality, mercy, and humility in his Beloved, and he found them greater and nobler when he contemplated them in himself. He said to Understanding that he could not fully grasp liberality, mercy, and humility in his Beloved. He said to his Will that his Beloved's mercy was so liberal that he could take from it as much humility as he needed, and have as much mercy and liberality as he needed for his salvation.

13. Blanquerna realized he was in danger of thinking that his Beloved's dominion was greater than His mercy and humility, because His dominion is over all people, and His mercy and humility extend only to those of the Catholic faith. The Beloved stirred Blanquerna's memory and reminded him that mercy caused the Son of God to humble Himself in the Incarnation and to die on the Cross. He did this so His dominion could be proclaimed through the world by those for whom God has humbled Himself in this Holy Sacrifice.

14. Blanquerna said that the princes of this world must have humility and patience when they exercise dominion, indicating that God should possess humility and patience in His dominion. Thus, as prince of his memory, understanding and will, Blanquerna

humbled himself so he might have patience and contemplate humility, dominion, and patience in his Beloved.

15. Blanquerna ended his prayer. On the next day, he returned to it, taking the virtues by three and three so that he could follow a new method. On the next day, he considered the virtues by four and four, by five and five, or by two and two, uniting them with Greatness or Eternity. In every such combination Blanquerna found more to contemplate in his Beloved. Because he followed an art of contemplation, Blanquerna so abounded in the contemplation of his Beloved that his eyes were always filled with tears, and his soul was filled with devotion, contrition, and love.

CHAPTER THREE
Of Essence

1. Blanquerna began to contemplate the Divine Essence together with the Divine virtues, and remembering, comprehending, and loving the virtues, he said:

2. "Divine Essence! Your goodness and eternity are so great that between Yourself and Your goodness, greatness, and eternity, there is no difference. You are Essence, You are God, for between Deity and God there is no difference. I adore You as One and the Same, as Deity and God, Essence and Being. If You were not One, without difference, Your greatness would be finite, inferior to Your goodness and Your good, Your eternity and eternal Being. I adore You and bless You in one pure and simple actuality with all Your virtues, since Your greatness is infinite in goodness and eternity.

3. "O glorious Essence, my soul remembers and comprehends of Your Goodness and Your good what it recalls of no other living thing. For goodness and good, greatness and great, abidingness and abiding are not one thing in creatures; if they were, there would be no difference between essence and being in creatures. Thus, to indicate the nobility of Your Being and Essence, Your Essence and Being are greater as One than created essence and created being, where greatness is lacking. Because of this lack, we grasp and know Your infinite greatness. I praise Your greatness, adoring, contemplating, and serving Your glorious Essence."

4. "Essence and power, knowledge, and will are distinct in the creature, for power is one virtue, knowledge another, and will yet another. But since there is no difference between Your power, knowledge, and will, O glorious Essence, You are therefore one Essence, and there is no difference between Your Being and Your power, knowledge, and will. Since this is so, You are Sovereign Good, since all other good lacks power, knowledge, and will that is one with its essence, and by nature tends toward corruption."

5. "O glorious Essence, Your power can cause no defect in Your Being. But, since my being is one thing, my essence one thing, and my power another, my power can cause defect in my being.

    But since Your power and Your Essence and Your Being are one, You can do nothing against Your Essence and Being.

    Because of this, O Essence, You have eternal power, infinite and complete, in truth, virtue, glory, and perfection."

6. "Justice is named for the just man, and wisdom is named for the wise man. You reside in Your Deity, O God; the one who speaks of Your Deity speaks of God, and the one who speaks of God speaks of Your Essence. Your Virtue is sufficient to be Your Essence in truth, glory, and perfection. There is greater truth that Your Being and Your Essence are One than that essence and being are not one in the creature, or that the just is one thing and justice another. Thus, many who are just, chivalrous, and human differ in various ways regarding justice, chivalry, and humanity. But

this is not so with Your Being and Essence, for there is truth and virtue in Your glory and perfection, and there is no diversity of Being and Essence."

7.   "If justice didn't exist in the creature, it would be impossible that the just man could be created. Before humanity and all this world existed, Your justice contained both justice and the 'just.' Just as humanity cannot be without the elements that make it human, there could not be justice or the just in Your Essence if it contained difference of Being and Essence."

8.   "Divine Essence! Before the creation of humans on whom You lavish Your gifts, liberality was a part of You. If You are liberality and liberality is Yourself, Your liberality is no way less than Your Essence in Your Eternity and Infinity.

The same is true of Your mercy and the remaining virtues.

Your mercy and liberality are not now any greater when there are creatures on whom You lavish Your mercy and forgiveness.

If there were a difference in Your Essence between mercy and liberality, then You would not have been merciful or liberal until You created the world. But it is impossible that You would have created any thing if Your Essence didn't already contain mercy and liberality."

9.   Blanquerna reflected that humility, dominion, and patience are qualities in creatures, but these virtues are in God's Essence. So Blanquerna adored humility, devotion, and patience as Divine Essence and Being. He said: "Humility that does not humble, dominion

that has no domain, and patience that is not patient cannot be Sovereign Essence in goodness and greatness." While Blanquerna contemplated in this way, he grew troubled and was afraid he might utter a contradiction. But, because his understanding had risen to such great heights in his contemplation, Blanquerna's memory recalled that all good things in the creatures must be attributed to God, because they all must be contained already in the Divine Essence, for there are no imperfections in God. Since humility, dominion, and patience are good things in the creature, so they must be the same in the Divine Essence. Since creatures do not possess humility, dominion, and patience in as great perfection as God, we must understand that in another and a nobler way, humility, dominion, and patience are in the Divine Essence—a way unlike that in which they exist in the creature, where they have beginning and end.

10. As he contemplated, Blanquerna said that his Beloved's Essence is immovable, because He comprehends and is not comprehended. He is unchangeable, because He is eternal. He is incorruptible, because His power, His will, His knowledge, His virtue, His perfection, and His justice are eternal. Thus, Blanquerna strove to remember his Beloved's glorious Essence in his understanding and will more than any other essence or essences.

11. "The king, with all his dominion, strength, beauty, wisdom, power, and justice possesses no more human essence than one of his servants, a poor man who pos-

sesses little power and knowledge, because the king may lose all his virtues at any time. But this is not so with God's Essence and His virtues, for this Essence and these virtues are one and the same in goodness, greatness, eternity. No other thing may have God's virtues nor be His Essence. Thus, the Divine Essence is in virtue, in presence, in wisdom, in power, and in all that pertains to His Essence, in every place and through every place, in every time and through every time."

12. In this and many other ways Blanquerna contemplated God's Essence, uniting virtues with others so he might make lengthier matter for the contemplation of His Essence.

When he had ended his prayer, he wrote down the substance of his contemplation, and read it after he wrote it. While he was reading it, though, he had less devotion than when he was engaged in contemplation. Thus, less devout contemplation will result from reading this book than from contemplating its substance, for in contemplation the soul soars higher in remembrance, understanding, and love of the Divine Essence. Devotion conforms more to contemplation than to writing.

CHAPTER FOUR
Of Unity

1. Blanquerna turned his reflections and love to the contemplation of God's unity. He said: "Sovereign Good! Your Goodness is alone in its infinite greatness and its eternity and in power, for there is no other goodness that can be infinite, eternal, and of infinite power. Therefore, O Sovereign Good, I adore You alone in one God Who is Sovereign in all perfections. You are the only Good from which all other good springs. Your Good alone sustains all other good. Your Good alone is the source of my good, so all my good devotes itself to the honor, praise, and service of Your Good alone."

2. "O Loving Lord! Greatness that is without beginning and end in Your Essence full of virtue and complete in perfection, You conform to one God alone and not to many, because eternity that is without beginning and end conforms well to greatness, which in essence and virtue has neither beginning nor end, but is itself both beginning and end in all its fullness. If this weren't so, O Lord, it would mean that justice and perfection would be contrary qualities in eternity. Since You, my God, are One with Your justice and perfection, my understanding grasps You as One God eternal and alone."

3. Blanquerna's memory remembered God's goodness, greatness, eternity, wisdom, will, and power. By His goodness, he understood a power possessing more

goodness than any other; by His greatness, a power that was greater; by eternity, a power more abiding; by wisdom, a power more wise; by will, a power more gracious than any other power. Thus, when the understanding had comprehended the Divine power, the memory reflected upon one power alone, above all other Sovereign, and, therefore, the understanding grasped that God was One and One only. For if there were many gods, it would be impossible for the understanding to comprehend a greater and nobler power than all others.

4. Blanquerna reflected upon the virtue that is in all natural things, and he grasped that in every natural thing there is one virtue that is lord over the other virtues. While Blanquerna reflected upon these things, his memory carried his understanding to grasp the end for which all humanity is created, and how beasts, birds, plants, metals, elements, heavens, and stars have one end only, to serve humanity. Thus, according to the perfection of power, justice, wisdom, and will, all humanity is to honor and to serve one God alone. For, if there were many gods, each god, according to his perfection and justice and power, knowledge and will, would have created humanity and creatures for many ends. As Blanquerna contemplated God's unity in this manner, he felt himself greatly uplifted in his memory and understanding and will.

5. Man is given will, and he wills to possess for himself alone his castle or his city or his kingdom, or his possessions or his wife or his son, or his memory or his understanding or his will. When Blanquerna had

remembered this, he remembered God's glory and dominion, and grasped that if there were many gods and lords of the world, their glory and dominion could not be as great as that of one God alone.

Since to God must be attributed the highest glory and dominion, Blanquerna understood that God is One and One only. So his understanding might rise to greater heights of comprehension, his will was greatly exalted in fervor to the contemplation of his Beloved, the Spouse of his Will.

6.   Blanquerna said: "It is true, O Lord God, that there is no other God except You alone. To You alone I offer myself to serve You. From You alone I hope for forgiveness, for there is no other liberality nor mercy to forgive, except Yours. Humble I am if I humble myself to You. Lord I am, if I am Yours alone. I have victory over my enemies if I suffer for You. With all that I am, a guilty sinner, I give myself to You alone, and Yours alone I am. Of You alone I beg forgiveness, in You I trust, and for You I endure trials. Whatever may happen to me, let it all be to the one end of Your praise, honor, and glory. I will have no other Lord, for You alone I fear, from You alone comes my strength, for You I weep, for You I burn with love."

CHAPTER FIVE
Of Trinity

1. Blanquerna wished to contemplate the holy Trinity of our Lord God. So he begged God that He would exalt the powers of his soul so they would rise to the contemplation of His virtues and contemplate His glorious Trinity. Thus he said: "Divine Essence, glorious and holy, in Whom is the Trinity of Divine Persons! I ask You for Your favor, that You may be pleased to humble Yourself so my soul may rise to contemplate Your Trinity with Your virtues, proper, essential, and common to three Persons, and Your three properties, personal and essential. I am not worthy to ask or receive this favor. But since You can grant it, and because of this knowledge I can better love, know, and praise You—for this reason, I ask this of You. For my soul desires to know and love all these things, that it may better love, know, praise, and serve You and make Your glories and honors loved and known."

2. Blanquerna trusted in God's help and said: "Infinite and eternal Good was never in creatures, because all created good is finite and determined in greatness and eternity. If in the creature there were a Good that was infinitely great in eternity, knowledge, power, and will, it would indeed be possible that one infinite Good should generate another; for, if this weren't so, it would be impossible that creatures would possess such an infinite Good." When Blanquerna had committed this to his memory, understanding, and love,

he remembered and understood that if the Sovereign Good exceeds created good in greatness, eternity, power, knowledge, and love, It must have as well a higher and nobler work and actuality. For, if It did not have this it would be impossible that It should exceed created good in infinity of goodness, greatness, eternity, power, and wisdom.

3. When Blanquerna, with God's help, had lifted up his soul's powers to a high degree, he strove to lift them even higher. He reflected upon how great a good it is that God should be generated, Who is Good, infinite and eternal, powerful, wise, loving, virtuous, true, glorious, perfect, just, liberal, merciful, humble, patient, and Lord over all things. When he had reflected upon these things for a great while, he thought again how great a good it is that all these virtues that are common to the Persons of the Trinity should be attributed to God. He again reflected on how great is that Good that generates God, and the eternal and infinite from which God proceeds. When Blanquerna had considered all these things, he used the method of negation to reflect upon how the good about which he had thought might not be in the Sovereign Good. Immediately, his soul was empty of devotion and understanding. So, using the method of affirmation, he reflected upon the virtues of God and the Trinity, and his soul was filled with remembrance, understanding, and love of the Sovereign Good. Thus, he began weeping and praising God Who had granted him so high a degree of contemplation.

4. God's perfect justice, wisdom, glory, and truth indi-

cated to Blanquerna that the world had had a beginning and that the work of Divine Essence in Itself, out of which the Father generated the Son and the Holy Spirit proceeded from the Father and the Son, is an infinite, eternal, and wholly perfect work. If this weren't so, it would follow that the world, in receiving eternity, would have as much infinite virtue as the Divine Power has in giving out virtue eternally, and this is impossible. When this impossibility was revealed to Blanquerna, his understanding was so greatly exalted that his will soared high in love to the Trinity. The love gave afflictions to his body, tears to his eyes, sighing and devotion to his heart, and prayers and praises of his glorious God to his mouth.

5. Fearfully Blanquerna said these words to the Holy Trinity: "Sovereign Trinity All Excelling, through Your common virtues my understanding soars so it may contemplate and love You, and in Your virtues, personal and proper, my understanding fails me when it has knowledge of You. But my will, illumined by the light of faith through Your blessing, soars to love You. Thus, I am contemplating You through intellect and faith without there being any contradiction."

6. While Blanquerna contemplated the Sovereign Trinity, Error and Ignorance inclined him not to believe any longer in God's Trinity, and he considered how in all trinity there is a certain structure. Then Blanquerna reflected once again upon the infinite greatness in power, perfection, and eternity, and grasped how, if created plurality and eternity must have such structure, then the Sovereign Trinity must

have a greater structure. For, as the Sovereign Trinity and Plurality is superior to created plurality and trinity in goodness, greatness, eternity, and power, It is above it also in simplicity. For if the Unity of God is in simplicity Sovereign over all created unity, the Sovereign Good must have plurality so It may be in simplicity above created plurality.

7.   "O Holy Trinity! Inasmuch as I do not grasp You, my understanding is less than Your greatness. Inasmuch as I believe without grasping You, my faith is greater than my understanding and Your greatness greater than my faith.

This is so because Your greatness is infinite in all perfection, and my faith and understanding are limited and bound by Your greatness. Since by believing in You I am greater by faith than by understanding, if I understood You, I would be greater in loving than in believing. If this were not so, it would mean that love conformed more to ignorance than to understanding, which would mean love would be less in the heights of understanding. This is impossible since there exists a great diversity of objects between faith and understanding. This diversity exists in the Divine virtues that are held in common by all three Divine Persons."

8.   Using the art of contemplation, Blanquerna reflected upon generation in infinity and eternity, so he might not think Divine generation is like that of the creatures, which he could not conceive in his mind to be a thing of infinity and eternity. Thus, he grasped in Sovereign generation simplicity without creation or

corruption. He could not believe that there was neither corruption nor creation in the lower generation, because his understanding knew that the generation of the creature cannot increase perfection in eternity and infinity.

9. "O Holy Trinity! If You didn't exist, how would God be like humanity? Or, how could the words, 'Let us make man in our image and likeness,' be true? If You, O Trinity, are unlike any trinity of ours, it is because You are a Being infinite and eternal in Wisdom, Power, and Perfection." Thus did Blanquerna contemplate the Holy Trinity, and he lifted up the powers of his soul so he might obey God's commandment that exhorts one to love God with all one's strength, with all one's mind, and with all one's soul, that is, with memory, intellect, and will.

CHAPTER SIX
Of Incarnation

1. Blanquerna remembered the Holy Trinity so his understanding might grasp how, through the influence of the glorious Trinity's great goodness of eternity, power, wisdom, and will, God should perform in the creature a work of great benevolence, eternality, power, wisdom, and charity. Because of this, his understanding grasped that, according to the operation of the Divine Persons, it was fitting God should become human, so He might show forth His Divine virtues and the works He has in His Divine Persons, and so the wills of Blanquerna and all humanity might love God and His works.

2. "Divine Virtue," said Blanquerna, "You are infinite in goodness, greatness, eternity, power, wisdom, love, and all perfection. Inasmuch as all virtue is finite, except Yours, there is neither in eternity nor in infinite greatness any thing sufficient to receive Your work. In order to show forth these things, Your wisdom willed to create a creature greater in goodness and virtue than all other creatures and virtues created, and the Son of God willed to be one Person with that creature, to show that Your goodness had been able to give Him greater virtue than all other creatures, even though He could make Him greater than all other creatures."

3. "Your humanity, O Lord, has a glory greater than all other created glories, because its perfection surpasses

all other perfection. Since Your justice, O Lord, has greater goodness, power, love, wisdom, and love than any other, it was willing to give greater glory and perfection to Your humanity than to any other created thing. Since this is so, it is fitting that all the angels, all the souls of the saints, and all the bodies of the just when the resurrection is past, should have glory in Your humanity and thus rise to have greater glory in Your Divine Nature."

4. When Blanquerna had reflected on these things a great while, his memory, understanding, and will were greatly uplifted in contemplation. Even so, his heart did not give tears to his eyes. So Blanquerna prepared to lift the powers of his soul higher so they might multiply devotion even more in his heart and fill his eyes with weeping and tears, for high contemplation needs to be accompanied by weeping. Thus, Blanquerna caused his memory to descend and to reflect upon the vileness and the misery of this world and its sins.

He contemplated also the great wickedness committed against our Creator by Adam's disobedience and God's great mercy, liberality, humility, and patience, for it pleased God to take human flesh, and He willed to give His Body to poverty, scorn, torments, and trials, and to a vile and grievous death, although He had no guilt or sin like ours.

When Blanquerna called these things to mind, the will had so much devotion from the nobility of the virtues and the Passion and Death of the Nature of Jesus Christ, that it gave the heart sighs and griefs, and the heart gave weeping and tears to the eyes, and to the mouth it gave confession and praise of God.

5. For a long time, Blanquerna wept as he contemplated the Incarnation of the Son of God. But as he wept, he could not imagine how the Son of God conformed Himself to human nature. Since he could not imagine this, his understanding no longer had knowledge, and he began to doubt. Because of his doubting, his tears and sighs ceased, and his devotion was destroyed. When Blanquerna realized how low his thoughts had sunk, he lifted up his memory and understanding to the greatness of God's goodness, power, wisdom, and perfection.

    In the greatness of these virtues his understanding grasped that God may conform Himself to human nature, even though the imagination may not know or imagine it. God's goodness, power, wisdom, and will are greater than the imagination's imagining. Thus, through memory and understanding Blanquerna destroyed his doubts about the Incarnation. Devotion and contrition returned to his heart, and weeping and tears returned to his eyes. His contemplation was loftier and more fervent than at the beginning.

6. Blanquerna continued to contemplate the Incarnation of the Son of God. Blanquerna remembered how the holy Incarnation and Passion of the Son of God are honored in God's goodness, greatness, eternity, and power, and how in this world He has honored with His grace many who do not honor Him as they might. After this, he remembered how many people in this world are unbelievers and do not honor the human

nature of Jesus Christ which God in Himself has so greatly honored.

God took that human nature and, to honor us and restore us to the Sovereign dominion we had lost, He suffered Passion and Death. Then, after Blanquerna had fixed his powers of mind upon that matter, his devotions, sighs, tears, and griefs were renewed within him, and his mind soared higher and higher in contemplating the sacred Incarnation of the Son of God.

Thus, he said: "O Lord God, Who have so highly honored and exalted our nature in Your Divine virtues! In Your holy Incarnation and Passion You honor our remembrance, understanding, and will."

7. So lofty was Blanquerna's contemplation that the powers of his soul conversed with one another in his mind. Memory said that great goodness performed a great work, and great power worked great might. Understanding answered that great mercy, humility, liberality, and love conformed lesser virtues to greater ones. And Will said that above all creatures he loves his Lord Jesus Christ. At one thing he marvelled, though. How is it, he wondered, that when Jesus Christ so greatly loved His people, willed to suffer for them, and when God greatly willed to humble Himself, that there could be so many people who are unbelievers and ignorant of His honor? Understanding asked Will how it should have such devotion as to make people desire martyrdom to honor the Incarnation. Memory wondered how it should have such lofty remembrance of God's virtues that He

might be exalted in such ways as should demonstrate to unbelievers the sacred Incarnation and Passion of the Lord Jesus Christ.

8.   Blanquerna's Spirit was illumined and inflamed by the Divine Light of the spirit. He said: "O Incarnation, O greatest truth of all truths, uncreated and created! Why are the numbers of men who scorn you and do not believe in you greater than the numbers who honor and believe in you? What will you do? Will you punish so great and mortal failings? O mercy that possesses such great benevolence, love, patience, and humility! Will you forgive them?"

So Blanquerna wept, and between fear and hope he had sorrow and joy as he contemplated the sacred Incarnation of the Son of God.

CHAPTER SEVEN
Of the Pater Noster

1. Blanquerna remembered the Divine Virtues, and through them he began to contemplate God in the Pater Noster and to set the virtues and the Pater Noster in his memory, understanding, and will. He spoke to God: "O Father, You are our Lord. God the Father is Father of God the Son, Who is infinite and eternal in goodness, power, wisdom, love, perfection, and all His other attributes. Your Divine Essence is Father of the humanity of Jesus Christ by creation and by benevolence, mercy, liberality, humility, and love. Thus, Jesus Christ said, when He prayed the Pater Noster, that in You is the personal Father of God the Son, and that You are that Essence, which is the Father of His humanity and of all other creatures. Because the Apostles were creatures, and because they believed in His Trinity and Incarnation, our Lord Jesus Christ commanded them to say the Pater Noster."

2. "You, O Lord, are in the heavens God the Father of God the Son. The heavens are Your infinite greatness, goodness, eternity, power, wisdom, and love, and these are Essence in which lies God the Father, Who conceived God the Son. Since infinite perfection is in Your Essence in goodness, greatness, and eternity, the heavens may be compared with Your virtues, which are so high that no other virtues except Yours are sufficient to reach such exceedingly great heights. By virtue of these heights You make it known in the

Pater Noster that You are Father, because You are higher than all creatures, and because in Your heavens are Your works, so that Jesus Christ called You His Father and our Father. If Jesus Christ, Who is God and Man, bears witness that You are His Father and ours and is in the heavens, it is fitting that we should believe His witness and say the Pater Noster."

3.   "Blessed be Your holy and glorious Name, O Lord God, which is the Name of the Father, Son, and Holy Spirit. Since the Father is eternal, the Son eternal, and the Holy Spirit eternal, and each one of these Persons is infinite in perfection, there are in Your Essence Names eternal and infinite and perfect. It is fitting, then, that Your personal Names should be blessed in Your Divine Essence, eternal, infinite, and complete."

4.   "It is fitting that Your Name should be blessed among everyone throughout the world. Therefore, You have established the Holy Roman Catholic Church, so Your Name may be named and known throughout the world and blessed in people's souls and blessed in the holy Sacrament of the Altar."

5.   "Your Kingdom, O Lord, is Your very Essence and Your personal properties, in which lie goodness, greatness, and eternity. May that Kingdom come, O Lord, to our souls through remembrance, understanding, and love of Your universal properties and Your own personal properties, so Your Kingdom may be honored among us here below and so we may rise to live perpetually in Your glorious Kingdom."

6.   "Your will is done, O Lord, in the heavens and on earth." This will is done in heaven because Your

Essence is goodness, and goodness and will come from the inifinite Father and Son in goodness, greatness, and eternity. Your will is perfected in the Son. Thus, it is the will of justice, perfection, virtue, and truth that Your will be done on earth. This Will was done by the work of the Holy Spirit when He gave You flesh in the womb of the glorious Virgin."

7. "O Lord, Your Will is so lofty and marvelous that throughout this world You are to be obeyed through Your goodness and Your power, Your justice and Your perfection. You are obeyed through Your goodness, humility, patience, and mercy by those who desire to serve You and by those who withdraw their memory, understanding, and love from the world so they may contemplate and serve You. Those who fix their remembrance, understanding, and will upon earthly vanities and despise Heaven's blessings are punished with the pains of hell."

8. "Our daily bread, O Lord, is Your sacred and glorious Body sacrificed upon the Altar. Your Body is in the heavens, yet daily It is among us here on earth in this Sacrifice, which we are able to grasp because of the working of Your great benevolence, wisdom, power, humility, mercy, and will. Our eyes and other senses fail us when we see this Bread, so we ask that the powers of the soul will be sufficient, with Your help, to see this Bread through the working of the virtues of Your Essence. If Your benevolence, humility, will, and liberality are infinitely great according to Your perfect justice, it follows that You will give us our daily bread in this world."

9.   "Forgive us, O Lord, the debt we owe You, for we can never pay You, since we are all sinners. So great are our debts to You that we can never pay You, for You created us and willed to become Man, to be tortured, crucified for us, and to die, because You loved us so much. Since Your perfection is infinite in Your goodness, greatness, and eternity, You don't need us to pay You. If You needed that payment, You would lack perfection. Since we forgive the debts we owe our sensual natures with fastings, afflictions, and prayers, if You didn't forgive us our debts, as we for Your love forgive our debtors, we would have greater justice and perfection than You. But this may not be. So it is fitting that You should not require of us our debts, which we could not pay You."

10.   "We know, O Lord, that Your great goodness, love, mercy, and liberality make You desire us to have great merit, so Your justice may give us great glory and perfection. Thus, You allow us to be tempted by the world, the flesh, and the devil. Since we are poor in memory, understanding, and love, we are often overcome by our temptations. But You in Your great benevolence, mercy, liberality, and humility give to us what we do not deserve if we endure our temptations. It is sufficient that we are in Your kingdom and have Your glory even without our own merits."

11.   "Deliver us, O Lord, from the evil that comes from not knowing You, not loving You, or forgetting You. This deliverance comes through remembrance, understanding, and love of Your goodness, greatness, eternity, and power."

In this way, and in many others, Blanquerna contemplated in his soul the virtues of God together with the Pater Noster.

CHAPTER EIGHT
Of Ave Maria

1. Blanquerna contemplated the Queen of Heaven with the virtues of her glorious Son, our Lord God. Thus he spoke: "Hail, Mary! The goodness of your Son, Who is infinitely great in eternity, power, wisdom, and love, salutes you. The Son of God took your nature, yet He is one Person only, equal in goodness, greatness, and eternity to the Father and the Holy Spirit and to all essence in goodness and virtue."

2. "Full of grace! Power, Knowledge, and Will, which are one power, knowledge, and will in essence, have been incarnated in Flesh of your flesh and Blood of your blood. This Power, Knowledge, and Will is one Son and one only of the Sovereign Father. Thus, O Queen, you are filled with grace through the Son of God, and your Son that is Man. The Son that is God is your Son. Since this is so, you are full of grace because of the inflowing of your Son's full grace. From the fullness of your grace comes an inflowing to the memory, understanding, and will, which contemplate the fullness of your grace. Blessed then, O Queen, be your grace, which is so full that it fills all those who through such fullness will attain perpetual fulfillment."

3. "The Lord—namely Virtue, Truth, and Glory—is with you, O Queen. This Virtue, Truth, and Glory have infinity in power, knowledge, and will. This infinity is Sovereign Good in eternity. The Lord within you,

O Queen, enables you to be great in virtue and truth, you who after your Son are pre-eminent in virtue, truth, and glory over all other creatures. The Lord is in no creature so virtuously, truly, and gloriously as in you, for He has given no other creature such power to receive His virtue. Thus, since by His virtue you can receive greater virtue than any other creature, His glory is more truly in you than in any other creature."

4. "Blessed are you among women, O Queen, for you are given greater perfection, greater justice, and greater liberality than any other woman, all the angels, and all other creatures. The perfection, justice, and liberality given to you are Christ your Son, Who is perfection of all other perfection, justice of all other justice, and liberality of all other liberality. From this perfection, O Queen, you are blessed above all women, since you have more perfection than them all. Because you have so much perfection, justice and liberality will that you give perfection to every soul— in its remembrance if it remembers you, in its understanding if it understands you, and in its will if it loves you."

5. "Blessed is the fruit of your womb, O Queen. Mercy and humility have united that fruit with the Divine Nature to conceive a union greater than any other between God and His creatures. For this your Son, glorious Man, is Man in the Son of the glorious God, Who makes Him to be Man, while He is Himself one Person, namely God and Man. That Person, Who is God, and is infinite mercy and humility in goodness, eternity, power, wisdom, and love, has blessed your

Son in His being one with infinity of mercy, humility, goodness, eternity, and power. Since this is so, what fruit may be so blessed or more blessed than the fruit of your womb?"

6. "O Queen, the sun's brightness is so great that it gives light to the moon and the stars. Since your Son's mercy and humility are greater than the sun's brightness, the blessing given us from the fruit of your womb is brighter than the sun. Since mercy and humility have so greatly exalted your Fruit, it is right for you to remember us according to your greatness in mercy and humility. If mercy has been pleased to honor you, by your mercy be pleased to honor us. If humility came to you so you might be exalted, so exalt us that we may rise and receive the blessing of your womb."

7. "The Holy Spirit has come upon you, O Queen, and has overshadowed you with the power of the Most High. He has overshadowed you with a virtue that embraces all virtues. Because He has thus overshadowed you, you are the mother of every virtue and of all created virtues. All these derive brightness from your shadow, and through your shadow they are guided to the Son's brightness. Your shadow gives eternal shade to the Saints in glory and shields them from the perpetual fire."

8. "O Queen of Heaven! For two reasons your Son is Lord over every creature: first, He is God; second, He is Man conformed to God and made one with Him. As the Son is doubly Lord of the world, you are the most important woman in the world for two reasons:

first, you are Mother of God; second, you are Mother of the Man Who is made one Person with God. Because this is so, remember your special place, so He Who has placed you there may be pleased and that we may be exalted in the nobility of His dominion."

9. Thus in the Ave Maria Blanquerna contemplated Our Lady with the virtues of her Son. While he contemplated, his remembrance, understanding, and will were so exalted that he didn't know whether he was weeping or not. When he ended his contemplation, he knew his heart had given his eyes no tears. Since it was not fitting for him to contemplate Our Lady without weeping, Blanquerna began contemplating her again by remembering the patience of her glorious Son on the day when He was stripped of His garments, spat upon, beaten, crowned with thorns, nailed to the Cross, wounded, and killed. He remembered how Our Lady loved Him, and that, while men tormented Him, He looked upon her, and she upon Him, with sweet and devout looks. While Blanquerna contemplated these things, and led the powers of his soul to consider the virtues of God and Our Lady, his heart was so moved to devotion that his eyes had an abundance of weeping and tears.

CHAPTER NINE
Of the Commandments

1. Blanquerna remembered in the Gospels Jesus' answer about the Commandments, and he contemplated these with God's Divine Virtues. He said to his will: "You shall love your Lord God, for so you are commanded by God's goodness, greatness, and eternity. You are constrained to love, for God Who commands you is infinitely good and eternal. If you do not love, you are disobedient to infinite and eternal goodness. For such disobedience He will doom you to infinite and eternal affliction and torment."

2. The Understanding said to Blanquerna that God's power, wisdom, and love commanded the Will to love God with the whole heart.

3. While Blanquerna's Understanding reflected, the Will asked if it was permissible to love anything else besides God. The Understanding answered that the Will could love all created things if by loving them it might better love God.

4. As Blanquerna's Understanding and Will conversed, the Memory recalled how the Commandment says that people are to love God with all their souls. Being one of the three powers of the soul, Memory obliged itself to remember virtue, truth, and glory. Memory said to Understanding that she recalled how he was constrained to comprehend God's virtue, truth, and glory. Understanding was conscious of the many times he had failed to grasp God's virtue, truth, and

glory so that Will through faith should have greater merit. Thus, Understanding exalted himself to grasp God's virtue, truth, and glory, and sought forgiveness, because he through ignorance had gone astray, so that faith might be greater in Will.

5. Blanquerna said to God that His justice was perfect, and that His commandment must be just and perfect to all thought. Will said to Understanding that she— Will—set her love more firmly upon the greater part of that which Understanding comprehended when he comprehended with all his power. For the commandment is given to the whole of thought, which indicates all the power of understanding. As Will said these words, she became contrite, because she realized that she had not commanded Understanding to love God with all his power, as the commandment instructed. Memory then recalled that many people disobey God's commandment while thinking they are obeying it by exalting faith and denying the understanding.

6. Again Blanquerna considered God's commandment to the Will that people should love God with all their hearts, with all their souls, and with all their thoughts. God's command to people to love with all their hearts indicates faith, through which the will may love more than the understanding can comprehend. God's command to people to love Him with all their souls means that all three powers of the soul should be fixed equally on some end equally remembered, comprehended, and loved. God's command to people to love Him with all their thought indicates that He commands people to exalt their understand-

ing, that in remembering God the understanding
may have greater remembrance and in loving Him
greater will.

7. Blanquerna said to his soul that to love God with all
his heart and soul and thought is the first commandment. The understanding comprehended the second
commandment in relation to the first, for the second
commandment exhorted equality of love between
Blanquerna and his neighbor, in that God commands
the will that people should love their neighbor as
themselves.

8. To love, remember, and comprehend God above all,
and to love one's neighbor as oneself, are two commandments that are the beginning of all others.
Whoever obeys these two commandments obeys God
in all the rest; whoever disobeys God in any of the
other commandments disobeys Him in the first two;
and whoever loves one's neighbor and oneself equally
with God disobeys the first commandment and all
the rest.

CHAPTER TEN
Of the Miserere Mei Deus

1. Blanquerna contemplated God in His Essence and Trinity and Incarnation in the sayings of the holy Prophets. He said: "David begged God's forgiveness according to His mercy, and his soul reflected at the same time upon grace and mercy, goodness and eternity. God's goodness is greater than any other goodness, and His eternity greater than any other eternity. Since goodness and eternity conform with greatness, and God's mercy is greater than any other mercy, David sought goodness for the good of piety and forgiveness. He sought eternity so such forgiveness might be eternal and never-ending."

2. "David did not think it was fitting to make a distinction in God's Essence between greatness, mercy, and justice, for they are one. In praying that God would forgive him according to His great mercy, he recognized His great justice. For it characterizes great mercy according to great justice to forgive, and this indicates that it is greater justice that great mercy should forgive great faults and bestow great forgiveness, than that lesser mercy should grant forgiveness. If this were not so, it would follow that great mercy and great justice would not conform to one another."

3. When Blanquerna reflected upon these words, his soul rejoiced in his hope of God's mercy, justice, and greatness. He thus understood what great good, endless and eternal, is prepared for the person who asks

for mercy from God's greatness and justice. When Blanquerna had contemplated goodness, greatness, eternity, mercy, and justice, he contemplated these virtues in the three Divine Persons.

4. Blanquerna said: "O Lord God, Who are Father, great in Your power, knowledge, and will, because of Your goodness, mercy, and justice: Behold, David, in the person of the Roman Church, begs Your Son, Who is great in power, knowledge, and will by virtue of goodness, eternity, justice, and mercy. Because he asked You to have mercy according to Your greatness, You must have mercy with greatness as mighty as Your own, which we could only receive through Your glorious Son, Who is equal to Your greatness, and Whom You gave us in Incarnation and Redemption. Your Son points to Your glorious Trinity and Incarnation. Since Your Son is God, He is equal in virtue with Your greatness, and in Him and through Him You can forgive and judge."

5. Blanquerna remembered God's truth, glory, and perfection, and through David's words, he grasped that greatness conforms to truth, glory, and perfection, and that greatness is infinite. The fact that greatness and mercy are infinite virtues, and that David sought mercy according to God's greatness, indicates that the Son, in Whom is truth, glory, and perfection, asked the Father that His forgiveness might be equal to the Father's infinite grace. Thus, David sought God for His forgiveness in the person of Jesus Christ.

6. "Liberality, humility, dominion, and patience, O Lord God," Blanquerna said, "are infinitely great

virtues in You. For, if it were not so, David would have begged of You forgiveness that You could not have given because of a lack in Your virtues. Since it is impossible that You lack any perfection, Your liberality must have within it a gift proportionate to itself. In Your humility there must be the kind of humility in which all can humble themselves. Your dominion must have that which is proportionate to itself, so Your mercy, proportioned in the same way, may have a Lord Who can give. It is fitting that Your mercy should have patience in giving the same patience. If all this were so, then David might have asked for a Mercy greater than You could give, and this is unlikely."

7. Using this method, Blanquerna contemplated God in His Essence, Trinity, and Incarnation, explaining David's words together with the Divine virtues. By this art of contemplation people may uncover the secrets and dark sayings of the Prophets so the understanding might exalt itself to search God's deep things and increase its comprehension. Thus, in the heights of the understanding the will might be lifted up to love God greatly in His Essence, in His Trinity, in His Incarnation, and in all His works.

CHAPTER ELEVEN

Of the Seven Sacraments
Of Holy Church

1. Blanquerna contemplated God's virtues in the Sacraments of Holy Church. He said: "In the Holy Sacrament of Baptism, O Lord God, You demonstrate the greatness of Your power, knowledge, will, and virtue. For by great virtue of power, knowledge, and will You reveal to us the marvelous work of Baptism where, by water, the priest's word, and the sponsors' faith, the infant, who does not have understanding or will, is cleansed and purified from original sin in the Sacrament. This work, O Lord, is so much more marvelous than all works of nature that it points out how You have power, knowledge, and will to perform all that is Your good will and pleasure in supernatural ways."

2. "As in a city there are many offices, so in the city of Holy Mother Church there are the offices of the seven Sacraments. The seven Sacraments demonstrate the noble use that Your glorious virtues have in the creatures. The goodness and greatness of Your dominion, Lord, proves how all creatures are obedient in the seven Sacraments to Your power, knowledge, and will."

3. "Glorious God! As the infant has no eyes of reason until it is grown, the sponsors must possess the virtue which Your virtue gives to the infant when it reaches

the age of confirmation. That the sponsors should have such virtue, that at the child's confirmation their obligation should be fulfilled, and that the child should receive virtue through its confirmation by the Bishop, indicate the great virtue, truth, perfection, and dominion that in the Sacrament of Confirmation perform all that Your will demands, without the opposition of any other power, which is powerless against You."

4. Blanquerna contemplated the Holy Sacrifice of the Altar with the Divine Virtues. He directed the powers of his soul toward this contemplation so he might not be impeded by the will's remembrance nor by the disobedience of the body.

5. Blanquerna said to the soul: "You know that God's humility is great, and His Power is equally great. Since humility and power are one thing in virtue with wisdom, will, truth, and perfection, the eyes are not very likely to be disobedient to the Divine virtues, which are so great that they have power, will, and knowledge that beneath the form of bread there may be Very Flesh and Very Blood of the Body of Jesus Christ. If this were not so, the eyes would have more power than the soul. It would also follow that there would be a lack of greatness in God's virtues, and truth would conform better to bodily things than to spiritual things. But this is not fitting, since God is spiritual Essence and His virtues are spiritual, and the body and bodily things are corruptible."

6. For a long time, Blanquerna conversed in his mind with his soul's three powers. Understanding said that

he could grasp how God's great virtue and power could cause Very Flesh and Very Blood to be in the form of bread. But he didn't grasp the reason God willed to make the Sacrament nor why He needed to make it. Blanquerna replied to Understanding that he should unite in his comprehension God's great goodness, wisdom, love, perfection, humility, liberality, mercy, and patience to grasp how great is God's power in transubstantiation. Because in this work we may know that the nobility of the Divine virtues conforms best with greatness, virtue, and truth, we may grasp the reason God willed to create the Holy Sacrament of the Altar.

7. "Understanding, my friend," said Blanquerna, "strive in virtue, for you have more virtue in understanding than the eyes have in seeing or the taste and touch have in tasting and touching, for you see these senses fail daily in many things. Don't let yourself be conquered by the bodily senses, but defend yourself from them by the Divine virtues. Do you grasp how wondrous a work is the Trinity in God, and how far above nature is the Incarnation of the Son of God? To demonstrate the wonder of this work, God was pleased to institute the Holy Sacrifice, so we would remember daily the wondrous and supernatural work of the Divine virtues. For even as we physically make the sign of the figure of our Lord God Jesus Christ on the Cross, so in the Sacrifice of the Altar the sign of the miraculous and spiritual work of the Divine virtues is made."

8. Understanding considered deeply the words

Blanquerna spoke to him. He grasped that the imagination had long kept him from comprehending the Sacrament of the Altar by causing him to represent it to himself more powerfully in its physical aspects than as the work of his glorious God.

Thus, Understanding performed Blanquerna's words, and he soared aloft in adoration and contemplation of the Holy Sacrament of the Altar.

9. There was some debate between Blanquerna's Memory and his Understanding about which Sacrament was more opposed to the bodily senses—the Sacrament of the Altar or the Sacrament of Penance. For the Memory recalled that humanity has sinned against God, and that the Holy Apostolic Father is human, as are the ministers who absolve and forgive and give penance to other humans. Understanding said that the Sacrament of the Altar manifests itself in bodily and sensible form, having indeed bodily form, but a form invisible to the bodily senses. They debated this matter for a long time, and they asked Blanquerna for his judgment in the matter. Blanquerna said that the Sacraments were equally opposed to the senses, for the incorporeal Divine virtues created and instituted the two Sacraments to show their sovereignty over natural and created virtue.

10. Blanquerna said: "As the Divine virtue causes the virtue of Flesh and Blood to exist in the form of bread, so It also causes the virtue of forgiveness to exist in the form of a man, the priest. And, as the virtue of Flesh and Blood in the form of the Host belongs to God and not to the Host itself, so the

priest's virtue in forgiving belongs not to the priest but to God."

11. "Blanquerna," said Remembrance, "could you prove to me that since God has the power to make the Sacrament of Penance He has to will that this Sacrament should be, for God can do many things His Will desires not to perform." Blanquerna replied that just as God's great goodness, mercy, humility, and virtue are demonstrated in the sacrament of the Altar, so His great justice wills that the Sacrament of Penance exist. Thus, His Divine virtues may be revealed, and people may be directed in contrition, repentance, affliction, and hope, all of which could not happen without the Sacrament of Penance.

12. To indicate the order that exists in the three Divine Persons, and how by means of this order the Person of the Son came to take our human nature, and how lack of order does not fit Baptism and Confirmation, the Holy Sacrifice, Penance, Matrimony, and Unction, it is fitting that an Order of Priesthood orders each one of the Sacraments. This is pointed out in the Divine virtues and in the greatness according to which they are demonstrated to us.

13. Blanquerna reflected upon the Order of Matrimony. He realized that just as justice dictates differences in humanity, it is also fitting that a difference be made between a man and a woman, that chastity and virginity should be different from lust, and that from sensual things the powers of the soul may take order and arrangement so the commandments of Divine Sovereignty may be obeyed.

14. "In the Earthly Paradise," Memory said to Will, "God created matrimony, and because of the meaning of that matrimony He wills the Sacrament of Matrimony should exist in this world. For, if this were not so, God's wisdom and will would not unite with perfection in pointing to God's great glory in its conformity with justice, which opposes the irregular union between man and woman. Through such irregularity humanity is unworthy of God's glory, for it would be against both greatness and perfection if humanity, after irregular union between man and woman, received God's truth and glory. Divine Wisdom and Virtue would have placed greater virtue in the bodily elements that unite rightfully than in the wills of man and woman, so that children may be conceived and the human race preserved in this world."

15. Blanquerna remembered that in this world persons have a beginning, a middle, and an end, and to demonstrate God's eternal dominion, Divine Wisdom has ordained that at one's entrance into the world Baptism should be the first Sacrament and that Extreme Unction should be the last. One's obedience to the first sacrament and to the others between the first and the last demonstrate the submission under which people have lived in this world. Since justice has greater reason to judge one who is obedient to law, and mercy to forgive one by Confession, Contrition, Confirmation, and the other sacraments, God's great Justice and Sovereignty will that Extreme Unction may be a sacrament. Extreme Unction is a seal set upon all the other sacraments.

CHAPTER TWELVE
Of Virtues

1. Blanquerna remembered the seven virtues that many times had aided him against the Spirit of Evil, and he contemplated the Divine virtues that the seven virtues had revealed to him. He said: "O Faith, you are worthy of all love, and you are great in believing great things of God, and you are good, for by you people come to eternal happiness. Through the light of grace, you are illumined with Divine Wisdom. You love those things that are true, for the King of Heaven's love enables you to love His virtue and truth, His glory and perfection."

2. "O Faith, my friend! You believe in God, Unity of Essence and Trinity of Persons. It is a great thing to believe in things invisible, to believe that infinite Good is that which infinitely and eternally generated from infinite and eternal Good. Thus, O Faith so lovely, since you are great, my soul gives great thanks and great love to the Eternal Greatness and Goodness that has made you so great, and in your greatness has made me great."

3. "Because of You, O Faith, I believe that by great love, power, knowledge, humility, and mercy, the Son of God took flesh of our Lady Saint Mary and became one Person having human and Divine Natures. I believe these things because of the greatness and virtue, doctrine, mercy, and benevolence of the Sovereign Good. Thus, my soul is compelled to

remember, comprehend, love, honor, and serve the Divine virtues which you, O Faith, cause to shine in me with such great grace and such brightness."

4. Blanquerna conversed in his soul with Hope and said that of great things one should have great hope. One should desire and hope for great happiness from such great goodness, greatness, eternity, power, wisdom, love, virtue, truth, glory, perfection, justice, and liberality. It is impossible that from such great and noble things exceedingly great happiness should not flow to the lovers of the Divine virtues.

5. "Consider, O Hope, how great a thing it is that the Son of God should unite Himself with human nature and to suffer death and torment for us sinners, so that you may trust even more in the virtues of the Sovereign Good. See, O Hope, how God has created many great and various beautiful things. Since these things are so noble and great, it is fitting, O Hope, that you trust in goodness, greatness, eternity, and power for great blessings and graces."

6. "O Hope, if there were no Trinity or Incarnation, you could not hope for such blessings from God as you now can. And, if there were no Resurrection, you would be less than you are, for we would not see the love, nor the power, nor the mercy, humility, dominion, and patience that in God are so great, as we see when we believe the Resurrection is true. Thus, O Hope, you and I see, together with the Divine virtues, Resurrection, as well as the greatness of the Divine virtues together with the Resurrection. Therefore, O Faith and Hope, we are greater in you."

7. "O Divine Love, you have within yourself a Lover Who loves infinitely and eternally. From You shall come all graces. If in Your Essence there are three Persons, Beloved and Loving, Eternal and Infinite in power, knowledge, will, virtue, perfection, and glory, from that great inflowing of love in You so much will come to us here in this world that we shall love to honor and serve no one except You alone."

8. "It is the nature of good to generate more good, and it is the nature of power to generate more power, and the same is true of virtue, glory, and perfection. How can it be then, O Love, that we do not love you, who are infinite in goodness, eternity, wisdom, and power, more strongly? Where, O Love, is the agreement you have with liberality, mercy, humility, and patience? For with such an agreement, you must have pity in you, and in us there must be happiness, hope, and love."

9. "O Divine Justice! In You the just and justice are one and the same. Since You are the just and justice infinite in Being and Essence without difference, and since that justice and Being and Essence in You is goodness, eternity, power, wisdom, love, virtue, truth, glory, perfection, mercy, liberality, humility, dominion, and patience, it follows that You are just to us in mercy, humility, compassion, and patience. Because of You, we have justice, so we may live justly, praising, honoring, and serving You."

10. "O Divine Essence! Your great justice causes the Just, Infinite, and Eternal in goodness, power, wisdom, and compassion to generate Another Just, Infinite,

and Eternal in goodness, power, wisdom, and compassion, and from both of these Just Ones comes Another, Eternal and Infinite in goodness, power, wisdom, and compassion. Since this is so, Your justice was so influential that it made One like us to be one Person with One of Three that are in You. Thus, since from this great influx of justice that came to One of us with compassion, mercy, and humility, this influx will come to all of us so we may become just in loving, knowing, honoring, and serving You."

11. "I pray through Your power, knowledge, and will, O Lord God, for prudence, which You will give me according to Your benevolence, justice, and mercy. Because Your power and knowledge can provide me with prudence, and since I ask for prudence so I may love You, Your truth and justice should love my prudence, so I may know and love You and through this knowledge and love may praise, honor, obey, and serve You."

12. "O Greatness of justice! If You are just in Your punishment of sinners, You will exercise this justice better if You punish those who know Your Trinity and Incarnation and do not honor, love, and serve You, rather than punishing those who do not know Your Trinity and do not believe in the Incarnation because they do not know about it. And, if You have mercy, humility, and pity on us, You will exercise these better if we know and love You than if we disobey You because of ignorance. Since Your liberality conforms to Your will, which has created us to love and know You before all things, You will give to faithful

Christians and to unbelievers alike that we may know and love You."

13. "Ah, Temperance, my friend! I need you daily to protect me against my enemies, who hinder me from contemplating God, for Whose sake I have become a hermit. I beg you for the virtues of the Lord who created you, for I need you to serve these virtues. I have left father and mother, friends and wealth, so that as a hermit I may have company with you. Without Temperance one can not resist gluttony or drunkenness, even though one wears the garments of honesty or embraces the office of hermit or the religious life. And I cannot possess you without God's goodness, greatness, wisdom, power, love, virtue, humility, mercy, and liberality."

14. "O Temperance, one cannot remember, understand, or love God too much. By satiety of remembrance, understanding, and love, with weeping and fasting, afflictions and vigils, the body weakens, languishes, and dies, and the soul does not as fervently or continuously contemplate God's virtues. Thus, O Temperance, I need you in both body and spirit. Give yourself to me so you may possess me and rule me." In this way Blanquerna prayed for virtues so he could serve God.

CHAPTER THIRTEEN
Of Vices

1. Blanquerna remembered the seven deadly sins that throw into disorder the world created by God's virtues. Thus, Blanquerna asked Divine Goodness: "Sovereign Goodness, You are so great in virtue and perfection that You are above all creatures in eternity and nobility. From where do gluttony, lust, greed, sloth, pride, envy, and anger come? These seven beasts destroy, corrupt, and ruin the goodness of Your sovereign creation. Since You are so powerful, wise, loving, and virtuous, how can You permit so much evil, deception, error, affliction, and ignorance to be in the world through these seven demons?"

2. "If You, O Goodness, were evil or lacked good, these seven deadly sins might have come from You. But, since perfection is contrary to defect, and since all sin and evil must have a beginning, let Your Eternity, which existed before such a beginning, tell me from where sin and defect come."

3. Blanquerna contemplated Sovereign Goodness in greatness, eternity, power, wisdom, and love, and he felt Memory and Understanding conversing in his soul. Memory said to Understanding how she recalled that Will desired gluttony, lust, and their companions. Understanding answered that the desire for gluttony or lust or any other vice is born in the will. Thus, the will is to blame because it comes before the desire to sin, and through the desire to sin

the understanding, which comprehends sin, is to blame. Thus, the memory, which recalls all these things, is to blame. Since Memory, Understanding, and Will are creatures of Sovereign Goodness, and give occasion to remember, understand, and love sin, the goodness of God is justified, for the seven demons have their beginnings in the works of remembrance, understanding, and will.

4. "O Divine Wisdom, show me how I may crush the seven vices in my memory, understanding, and will." Then Memory recalled the Divine virtues; Understanding grasped the shortness of life in this world and the pains of hell; Will loved God and all His virtues, ceased to love sin and prayed for forgiveness, and despised this world's vanity. Blanquerna felt in his soul that his vices and sins were crushed through the working of his remembrance, understanding, and will.

5. Thus, Blanquerna said to Divine Wisdom: "O Sovereign Doctrine, from You comes virtue, from Your Power comes power, and from Your love comes desire to the soul to remember, comprehend, and love You. Wrongs and faults arise whenever memory forgets You, when understanding doesn't comprehend You, and when will fails to love You. Thus, O Sovereign Doctrine, be in my remembering, comprehending, and desiring, together with my memory, understanding, and will, so I may contemplate, remember, comprehend, and love Your virtues and cease to love vices, wrongs, and sins, and so Your praise, honor, and dominion may be daily in my memory, understanding, and will."

6. "O Sovereign Liberality and Mercy, You have given me memory to remember, understanding to comprehend, and will to love Your virtues. But these are not sufficient if You do not give me the seven virtues that are opposed to the seven deadly sins. I pray that You will give me remembrance, understanding, and will to remember, understand, and cease from loving gluttony, lust, and other vices. Thus, since Your power can give me all these things that I need, and since You have created me for all these things, I pray You to grant me gifts so all my powers may honor Your graces."

7. "O Glory and Perfection, to give power to sin is to provide the occasion for having faith, hope, compassion, and the other virtues. The gift of the power to have faith, hope, and love is a gift against gluttony, lust, and the other vices. Thus, I pray You will give me these virtues so You may enable me to remember, comprehend, and love Your graces, and to remember, comprehend, and cease to love my sins and the vain delights of this world." Blanquerna wept and sighed as he prayed for these gifts. God granted him what he desired, and Blanquerna thanked God with tears. Only God can explain Blanquerna's contemplation and devotion and the art of his contemplation.